The Wellness Diaries

My Journey out of Mental Illness
Through Nutrition and Lifestyle Change

Owen Staples

iUniverse, Inc.
Bloomington

THE WELLNESS DIARIES
MY JOURNEY OUT OF MENTAL ILLNESS THROUGH
NUTRITION AND LIFESTYLE CHANGE

iUniverse books may be ordered through booksellers or by contacting:

iUniverse
1663 Liberty Drive
Bloomington, IN 47403
www.iuniverse.com
1-800-Authors (1-800-288-4677)

ISBN: 978-1-4759-8740-9 (sc)
ISBN: 978-1-4759-8741-6 (e)

Library of Congress Control Number: 2013907556

Printed in the United States of America.

iUniverse rev. date: 4/22/2013

To the well-being of both people and planet

Table of Contents

**"Never doubt that a small group of thoughtful,
committed individuals can change the world.
Indeed, it is the only thing that ever has."
-Margaret Mead**

Introduction

Considering that as of April 2009, I had set a date, with a detailed plan to take my own life, it's hard for one to believe that I would be here now writing a book about my journey.

All stories have a beginning; sometimes, the beginning becomes the end or the two meet somewhere in between; or, one discovers that as with a circle, he could have gone backwards and taken a huge shortcut to what he now calls the beginning. It is then he realizes that it is not always clear where one ends and the other begins.

My story begins during a battle with mental illness in 2001, at age twenty-two. As with any journey, it is never done; one has never arrived. The landscape may change, the individual may grow stronger, shed a few things here or there, but one has never arrived. There is only a point at which the author decides to put his or her story "out." May 14th, 2011, is where this story ends, as far as what is in print. We never stop growing, learning, evolving. The only thing that may stop our progression is our conscious choice to do so. Everything is a choice.

This is that portion of my story: 2001 to May 14th, 2011.

I believe my story shows that health and happiness are a choice. I can't say that I set out to do this. It was sort of my reward for much hard work, and some trial and error on the way. I am now eager to share my experience, and the valued insights I learned throughout the journey with others. If all 6.5 billion people on Earth did what I have done, that is reclaimed their health by finding *their* point of balance, beginning from *their* beginning and not mine or their neighbor's yes, the world would be a better place.

If every individual were happy, healthy and at peace, then every individual's "problems" would resolve and disintegrate; This could have a global impact, as enough individuals found peace, the problems we see within our world would also resolve and disintegrate. If this sounds particularly bold, first, I have a question for you: Throughout history, was there ever an undertaking to create change for a better world that was not bold? Does progressive, positive change *ever* allow people, communities, societies, to continue "business as usual" and to continue doing what several generations before those questioning had done?

I have taken a different path. At times it was unpopular and uncertain, but through it, I have found happiness and health. I'm a regular man who gathered some facts, tried them, tracked them, and I have organized them here so that anyone interested may do the same. This is the compilation of all the facts and experiences of my journey, and I've presented them as accurately as possible.

Using the triangular model inspired by author Ernest Callenbach, that is, steps toward better health are also steps toward helping the environment, and the added bonus is some money saved. I have taken his theory a step further and have come up with a formula, even if by accident, that has worked wonders for me. I submit that a similar philosophy would work wonders for our world as well. I believe this concept has potential to heal individuals and help our Earth tremendously too.

Read my experiences; soak in the words, the laughter, and the tears. The choice to act or not is just that, a choice. It is up to every individual on our planet, beginning with you.

MY STORY (2001-2009)

"Begin anywhere you want, but begin somewhere.
If you need to, you can start at the beginning."
—Owen

Chapter 1

"There's Always An Excuse When You Need One." –311

"An Entomologist, what is *that?*"
"*I would study insects.*" I replied confidently.

The above was me in second grade. Now, I still occasionally hear the same question, "what is that?" when people ask what I do, and I tell them I am a botanist.

Truly, throughout my entire life there was no hiding my quirkiness. From my earliest memories, I was always interested in the natural world. Growing up, I was often known as the "nature boy". In third grade, I had earned a sizeable reputation, well-known for my knowledge about animals. People were generally able to laugh off, and in the end, appreciate my quirkiness. I was popular and generally liked by most of the children I went to school with. Growing up through high school, I had many friends.

However, more recently (2001) about the age of twenty-two, my cute quirkiness seemed to be getting out of control. I was often told by family members and friends that I seemed overly cautious, even paranoid. I was obsessed with working out, keeping fit, and the martial arts, and learning to defend myself. I had enrolled in self-defense classes and attended them obsessively. I even began to carry combat knives, and often a tactical baton with me everywhere I went. Throughout my martial arts training I had learned to use them adeptly, believing that one day I would need to use them in a life or death, self-defense situation. Fortunately, for me and others, I never had to.

Martial arts training was part of my regular workout routine. These were intense workouts that also included flexibility training, strength training with weights and heavy martial arts bags, including a seventy pound free-hanging punching bag, and "Bob," the martial arts training dummy, which had a free-standing base filled with over one-hundred-fifty pounds of water. He looked menacing and helped me to increase the intensity of every workout.

With obsessive focus I trained on "Bob" and the heavy bags. Martial arts training was three days per week; strength training was two. I stuck to my routine. If I were forced to skip a workout I became extremely irritable, holding in my anger and placing blame on those who I presumed were the cause of my having to skip it. I took the workouts very seriously, expecting someday to need the training to defend myself in what I believed at the time would be a personal attack in which, if I were not well enough prepared, it would cost me my life. The way I saw it, I was simply training for the inevitable attack ensuring that I was well enough prepared for this eventual confrontation.

I was often confronted by young males in public in "stare-downs" which is often referred to as "mad dogging." This is where eye contact is maintained until the "submissive" person, looks away. If neither party backs down or looks away, gestures become stronger and are often escalated to the point of a physical fight. I put every effort into not being bothered by these attempts of other men to pick fights with me, but bothered I was.

Deep down, my higher self knew that I was the bigger man for choosing not to engage, and for not allowing things to become physical and violent over a foolish game of dominance; but I always felt like the "chicken" for doing so. This only made me train harder, fueled by my constant use of restraint.

One particular time, when I was walking my dog Elvis, I passed by a neighborhood man who I knew. I also knew that I did not like him. In an attempt to "mad dog" me, he stared at me long and hard as we approached one another. Not willing to back down from the challenge, I stared back. Something snapped inside of me. Although somehow I refrained from losing my temper, it had come very close to a violent outbreak; so close in fact, that the thought was already in my mind, and I had already seen the outcome flash before me. I saw him lying on the ground after I would have been finished with him a few seconds later. Thankfully, somehow I managed to control this urge. He and I passed by one another without any violence; we only continued to stare at each other in silent hostility.

As if this were not disconcerting enough, at this particular time in my life I slept every night with a loaded gun. I was convinced that during sleep when I was more vulnerable, my attacker would sneak in and attack me. I was prepared for this sabotage.

On another occasion, during my college days after a night on the town, several of my friends were inquiring about my martial arts equipment strewn about my residence at the time. I was challenged by one of the younger men to spar with him. I agreed to do so. The fact that he would dare "challenge" me annoyed me greatly. When I saw him decked out in sparring equipment with his guards up, coming toward me, I felt threatened. His body language closely mimicked the attack which I had long been anticipating, and out of self-preservation, I lost all control. I landed a swift round-house kick as hard as I could to his ribs. *Please note: In martial arts training, sparring is supposed to be educational, a practice session to facilitate learning. A generous amount of control is expected.

He immediately doubled in pain and dropped to the ground. I dropped to the ground with him, in deep remorse. I was feeling terribly at how badly I hurt him. Still decked out in gloves, head and shin gear, I held him compassionately, asking him if he would be ok, while apologizing to him. In the back of my mind though, I was only slightly bothered at my loss of control.

This pattern of feeling the need to defend myself and/or think defensively in nearly every situation continued for months. It was intermingled with the occasional humorous night out in my college days, but was worsening with the passage of time.

One weekend night, I was with a few of my college friends, eating late meal at Denny's. The meal was typical Saturday night banter. We were laughing, there were jokes, and amongst a party of girls and guys, there was a pleasant blend of chemistry, flirtation, and jests. One of the girls asked why I was so obsessed with working out. I told her in my matter of fact style that I liked to stay in shape. I liked to feel and look good.

The young lady playfully hinted to having OCD, to which I humorously replied, "Probably."

There were other inquires as to my type of workouts, and when I told them of my heavy martial arts bags, the one girl announced that she wanted to see how high I could kick. The men did too, because they didn't believe my claims. Near the end of the evening as we were leaving the restaurant, the girl insisted that I demonstrate my high kicking skills. I thought it was a joke, but the entire table was now egging me on to demonstrate my high kick outside of Denny's. I felt confident, and agreed to do so.

Just outside the front door of a Denny's in the center of the city on a Saturday night, I stood by the flowerbed, and demonstrated my "high front kick." I paused proudly in my stance and threw my extended right leg straight into the air as I had done hundreds of times while in class and at home practicing. It was no sooner that I saw the black shoe on my right foot pointing directly toward the crescent moon, that I felt my back meet the ground.

I was laughing after a few seconds, realizing what had happened, followed by every person in our group, as well as some by-standers. I relished the moment, which was an excuse for the young lady to help me up, and beneath her laughter, hug me and ask if I were okay. I was laughing at myself and with everyone else, too hard to answer. We shared a side hug as we walked, both laughing. I looked behind me to the rest of the party, "No warm up time!" I could barely say between laughs. As we all walked to our vehicles, the laughter and comments continued.

"Yeah Owen, that was the best front kick I've ever seen!" One man was barely able to say.

"I thought you would be dead," one of the ladies said.

I was embarrassed for sure, but it was all part of the fun, and the classic end to a fun evening. Yes, for the duration of my friendship with those seven people, I never lived that one down.

I was able to balance fun and fear, especially in social situations, as the above story shows; I was often called the "center of attention" and "the life of the party," in addition to always being known as quirky.

However, over the next year, I was able to fight off everything but my own fears. This was apparent to everyone except me, and fear was clearly winning the fight over fun. Throughout that year I was to go through several jobs, being fired from each for various reasons. It was obvious that my behavior was worsening beyond just quirky.

At one particular time, I became angry with my college professor because he had downplayed my question. I thought he was intentionally 'blowing off' my question, disrespecting me. Although I didn't say anything or show my hostility, I deliberately held up the line of students who were waiting to ask him questions. I stood like a tree, coaxing the professor along, spitefully waiting for the respectful answer that I required. When I found it acceptable (and only then,) I thanked him for his time, and stopped blocking the line of students.

I was fired for everything from not being able to concentrate or follow directions, to preaching to my coworkers, to nearly brawling with the visitors of the establishment. I had therefore decided that a change in direction would be refreshing and healthy. I decided to go to school full time and postpone working for the time being.

Throughout this period of time however, I wasn't just an angry, hostile, tough guy. I had a soft side too. I often found myself extremely emotional and weeping in certain situations. I would be moved to tears at movies, or swept away by feelings of gratitude to the universe for special experiences I had been given, or for my faithful dog companions I had at the time, Elvis and Taz.

During the fall semester of September 2001, while attending the local university, I often drove to the nearby parking lot, where students waited for the shuttle bus. One particular late afternoon I stepped onto the bus, prepared to go home for the day. I observed how particularly crowded the bus was. I took my seat, and after a few more stops, the bus was totally packed. Most seats were taken, and many students were forced to stand.

I couldn't help but notice a young woman who was sitting alone on a bench seat, with three empty spaces on either side of her. I was sitting across from her, and with so many people standing, I couldn't figure out why those empty seats were not being taken. I could see that she seemed different. She was also overweight. In my mind, this was the reason no students wanted to sit next to her. I believed that I could sense her insecurity and pain, and also her dejection upon finding that no one would sit next to her. I wanted to help her feel more comfortable and at least temporarily distract her from her pain.

My mind began grabbing for ways that I could reach out to her; ways that I could in a sense, say: "It's ok. I like you just how you are." What could I do though? I knew it would be strange if I got up out of my seat and moved to sit in one of the three empty seats next to her. I sat there with my anxiety turning to anguish, as we approached the end of the bus ride. I sat there quickly trying to brain storm. I was trying to think of something that I could say or do that would perhaps brighten her day.

At this time, she noticed me looking at her. I tried smiling warmly, but in my distress for her it seemed strained. Any insecure feelings she had were only worsened by my strained gaze and smile, and although in reality she probably hardly noticed me, I believed she thought I was mocking her and that it would somehow have an enormous impact on her life. This made me feel even worse. Soon thereafter, the bus arrived at the parking lot and all the students, including myself, and the young woman quickly exited. Anxiety was building within me. I knew that the moment had passed me by and the timing was gone; even worse, I had only worsened her pain.

For most people, wanting to help others, whether stranger or acquaintance is fine, even admirable. However, I tended to go about this in ways that were odd and made people feel uneasy rather than helped. This was part of a type of "savior" complex, which had developed while I was ill.

I walked to my vehicle feeling like I had failed, feeling responsible for her emotions. I felt as if I had added to her pain in sending her negative energy. I watched her walk to her vehicle; and as she got into her car and drove away, any remaining slivers of positive emotions I had went also.

I felt terrible. I felt body-slammed. I felt helpless. I thought that I was the only one on the bus who sensed her pain, saw the opportunity to help her along her way, but failed. I felt this to my core. It was very real.

At this point, I wished and hoped that she wouldn't choose to do anything drastic or jump to any major conclusions. I also sent her all the love and positive energy that I could. I tried to visualize her shaking off negativity like water from a duck's back, and I envisioned her happy, healthy and successful in life.

I was hyper-focused on this event and could not shake it. I was mad at myself. As I began the drive home, my emotions from the experience became overwhelming. I found myself sobbing. At one point, I was crying so hard that I couldn't see to drive and thought I would crash. I thought, "If I get pulled over, I will look like a freak! What on earth will I say to the officer?"

I did arrive home, thankfully avoiding a pullover or an accident. It always seemed to be that I couldn't arrive quietly; I must make a scene. I hoped to sneak in discreetly and not be seen crying. However, I lived at my parent's house at the time and there was often a house full of people, family. I walked in the door, still crying and all the activity throughout the front room naturally paused to wonder.

Among the pauses, I heard comments of concern.

"Something's wrong with Owen."

A few followed me into the other room in an attempt to console me, to find out what was wrong. I had locked myself into a back bathroom, not wanting to be seen or talked to, still feeling like a failure, and feeling so frustrated that I seemed to be the only one on the bus who sensed the girl's pain, or even cared.

When I did come out of the bathroom willing to talk, I still couldn't because I was still too emotional to speak. I sat for some time, as my family surrounded me with their love but naturally, were unsure of what to say or do. (In my family, we are not overtly emotional, and rarely cry outwardly.) Several questions were asked, as some of my family attempted to console me.

"Did you crash your truck"?

I shook my head, no. As I sat in the chair, my arms were crossed with my left hand resting on my cheek. This was a sort of defensive discomfort.

"Did someone punch you?"

I shook my head.

When I was finally able to tell them, they seemed somewhat relieved that I was not hurt, but also surprised that I was so upset over a perfect stranger. It's true that by nature, I am more self-absorbed; however, I do feel compassion, and at times I feel stirred deeply for the welfare of others.

A few months later, I experienced something similar on the bus while attending the university, equally as emotional. Upon trying to explain these experiences to loved ones, my fixation behavior was appearing increasingly abnormal. Throughout my conversations about these experiences with people, I was hearing more frequently that I should consider therapy.

For a short time in 2001 I had a job at a local restaurant as a host. Discomfort grew among my co-workers because of my odd mannerisms and behavior. I was often tense and defensive as I led people to their assigned seats for their meals. I thought the men were "mad dogging" me. I thought the women they were with were prodding the men to challenge me. As you can imagine, I did not explain all so well the soup of the day! My behavior, coupled with tension and suspicion amongst my co-workers that I was a troublemaker, ensured that I didn't last long at my new job; in fact, it lasted only three weeks.

For years, I believed that a tattoo I got when I was fifteen years old had given me HIV. I lived my life fully believing that I had HIV. I even had myself tested—twice. Both times the test results were negative but this provided little comfort. I could not convince myself otherwise. I believed it was an inaccurate test. No logical argument could shake my fear.

My declining mental health was becoming clearer and more pronounced with the passage of time, especially through the eyes of those who were most often exposed to my bizarre behavior. Since the first incident on the bus with the young lady, after months of gentle but steady encouragement and coaxing from loved ones to see a professional therapist, I finally agreed to do so.

On July 3rd 2001, I went to see a psychologist. I had agreed to do so if for nothing more than simply to vent about all of my frustrations with life. On the very first visit I felt comfortable venting out my frustrations and expressing my views. I was rather excited to "let it all hang out," especially to someone who would truly listen and possibly even have expert advice! I was in the process of explaining the basics of all my martial arts workouts. I had even wondered if I appeared normal enough that my therapist questioned why I was there. I wondered if I was perceived as quirky, at most.

I felt liberated, a weight off of my chest, as I informed my new therapist that I carried weapons with me in preparation for that final inevitable confrontation which I fully expected one day. It was the first time I had ever explained these fears to someone who was not family. In showing my therapist, Carol, I reached to the combat knife clipped onto my right pocket and pulled it out. Then I showed her the other one clipped to my left pocket, exposing the blades of each. (I can only imagine how alarming this must have been to my therapist!) In hindsight, it seemed as though my therapist was attempting to not appear alarmed although at the time,

I thought little of it. I was just explaining my routine of loading my pants pockets in the morning with keys, wallet, pocket watch, and two combat knives! My therapist remained calm and camouflaged any uneasiness she felt.

I really liked the prospect of venting my frustrations to a trained professional. I felt secure and confident, and that there was also a good level of trust on each side between my therapist and me. I scheduled a return appointment.

Always Into Animals

Animals always held a certain fascination for me, particularly reptiles. At this time in my life, they seemed essential to my well-being. They were therapeutic in and of themselves.

I had acquired a Chinese Water Dragon, "Rain" and a Bearded dragon, "Drakos", as animal companions. These two creatures I absolutely adored. I would spend hours at a time in my "rain forest room" (a combination of live houseplants and my reptile buddies) watching these wonders of nature, checking enclosure temperatures, feeding and watching them in the most natural of habitats that I could provide for them. To me, these creatures were far too often overlooked and I was grateful to provide for them spacious enclosures which often included live plants. Their enclosures were as elaborate and as spacious as I could possibly afford. During this period of attending university courses, keeping appointments with my therapist, and acknowledging my ever-growing fascination I had with reptiles and plants, I was learning much about myself and about life in general.

My therapist originally suspected that I had Obsessive Compulsive Disorder (OCD). I had also been diagnosed as having Attention Deficit Disorder (ADD) as a child and even as a young adult. I was taking medicines which were supposed to help me focus. However, somehow this medicine made me focus on strange things. It actually made me feel sort of invincible, and for "Mr. Martial Artist", "invincible" was not the best state for me; this was clearly not the appropriate medication for me at that time.

My therapist prescribed a few medicines, which were supposed to help me focus or relax more over a few weeks. I began one medicine to help with the symptoms of Obsessive Compulsive Disorder. The medicine felt like electricity was shooting through my entire body. To say that I had muscle spasms was quite the understatement. I could not sleep and I became extremely irritable while taking that particular medicine. I didn't like the medications and communicated this to my therapist who realized that the medicinal approach was not for me. Together, we decided to continue therapy without medication.

After about three months, we realized that my progress was especially slow through cognitive therapy alone, so my therapist wanted to try an entirely new approach. In November 2001, five months after beginning therapy, I agreed to take the Minnesota Multiphasic Personality Inventory (MMPI) test. This test is designed to more accurately narrow down a diagnosis for mental illness. I wanted to be accurately diagnosed so as to effectively treat my symptoms. I wanted to live a regular life.

When the results of my MMPI were in, my therapist encouraged me to come to the office with a few family members for support (in this case, my sister and mother) to hear the outcome of the test and discuss the outlook of the illness. My therapist calmly began to explain that the test results showed that I was suffering from a biological brain disorder or mental illness, known as Paranoid Schizophrenia.

I felt at first, emotionally as I had when a sparring partner kicked me square in the gut. It felt like such a blow, everything was taken out of me. I can sympathize, and I can see that this probably felt similarly to when someone is diagnosed with cancer, or diabetes. It took me a few seconds to "catch my breath" again. Then, I actually experienced a sort of relief; at least I finally had a name for it! So, between my recovery from the head on front kick to the gut, and my ironic sense of relief, I felt open, and largely hopeful.

Schizophrenia is a thought disorder, which affects a person's reasoning and judgment skills. People with this disorder are often quite paranoid and may experience auditory hallucinations such as voices or footsteps. A person with this disorder may also experience visual hallucinations. Another common symptom is delusional thinking, or false beliefs.

Schizophrenia is a serious illness and must be treated with anti-psychotic medication. Cognitive therapy in addition to medication is recommended by most professionals. This often includes re-training a person's thought patterns to promote more positive, harmonious thinking.

While therapy does little for the treatment of the illness itself, it does help to correct bad habits and behaviors learned while the person was ill. On the other hand, medications are used to balance serotonin and dopamine levels in the brain, helping to treat various symptoms of the illness, such as flattening emotion, or auditory or visual hallucinations. Medication and cognitive therapy combined typically act as an effective treatment of Schizophrenia.

The medications typically used are called anti-psychotics because they help to control psychotic symptoms. When a person is psychotic, they are in a state of psychosis, crisis. Psychosis means basically that the person is out of touch with reality and they are more than likely seeing or hearing things that are not there. They are often terrified. They are in crisis and they are acting from a state of delusional defensiveness. They are suffering greatly from the symptoms of their illness and need medication to treat the symptoms.

The name *Schizophrenia* can be misleading, however. The National Alliance on Mental Illness (NAMI), B.R.I.D.G.E.S manual provides clarification on this: "In 1911, a Swiss psychiatrist, Eugene Bleuler used the term Schizophrenia to describe the disorder he thought he was observing. (From Greek: schizo= to split and phren= mind) he thought the phrase described the split between reality and what a person in psychosis thinks, feels and senses about the world." Schizophrenia has nothing to do with the Split Personality Disorder. This disorder is actually entirely different.

I was rather alarmed at the uncertainty of my future having this illness. Only about a third of the people with this illness are able to live normal, productive, joyful lives. It was uncertain if I would ever be able to have long lasting, loving relationships, or hold a full time job, or even be able to work at all. It was a great possibility that I would never have a "normal life."

The more I found out about the illness, the more worried I became; but also the more open I felt to accepting treatment options. I wanted to live a normal life. The real possibility of me living in and out of jail, mental hospitals, and quite possibly not able to work, or sustain loving relationships absolutely terrified me. I had always wanted to marry, work, and live a normal life, as most people do. At age twenty-two, when those very things, (career, marriage, education), were at the center of all my hopes and desires, this was deflating news at best.

OWEN STAPLES

It was a long and draining day. I was encouraged to visit a psychiatrist immediately so as to begin taking anti-psychotic medications. I was referred to a local psychiatrist in the area, and it just so happened had a cancellation in appointments that day, and could fit me in. I wanted to begin medication right away rather than wait for two months until his next opening. I intended to give a normal life my "best shot." I drove to the office of my new psychiatrist. As my mom and I waited for the doctor to arrive, I was feeling tired and uncertain, in a sort of daze, and yet relieved to finally have some answers, new possibilities. Through it all, I felt receptive. When the doctor came out of his office, I heard him say to the receptionist, "So I have an hour with this person?"

I knew that he was referring to me, and I was immediately on the defensive that he would refer to me so impersonally as "this person". This made me think that he did not really care to see me, and that I was viewed as just a burden to him. During the session, I answered his questions, giving bits of detail. Just as I did with my therapist, I pulled out my knives to show him, explaining calmly why I carried them with me, believing that I would one day be attacked, and have to fight for my life. His voice changed and he became tense. He told me in a stern tone, "You know as well as I do that what you're doing is wrong."

Surprised and rather stunned at his harsh response, and immediately defensive, I became snappy, "What the hell am I doing wrong?" I felt extremely agitated. In a sense, I felt betrayed and attacked. I felt close to the point of aggression, as if I would explode in a violent attack, using fists, feet and knife. I felt explosive.

"Bringing knives with you;" he warned sternly, "and if you ever bring those into my office again, I will call the police." His eyes widened and his breathing was rapid. With thoughts of attacking him racing through my mind, I muttered several cuss words directed at him, but fortunately I refrained from violence.

I felt like his whole attitude toward me was too carefree, like I was just another "routine psycho" cluttering up his day. I felt very much on edge, defensive, and I left his office upset, swearing that I would never take any medicine prescribed by him; however, somehow, I did leave with a prescription in my hand.

As soon as I walked out of the office, I called my therapist's office leaving the message with the receptionist that I would definitely not take anything prescribed by that doctor who I thought of as weird, incompetent, and I believed him to be a porn addict. This was my first impression of him. That first visit, he gave me the willies. Over the years, I had grown to distrust anyone who had a porn obsession, and this was my impression of him—a porn addict disguised as a doctor, telling me to take the pills he prescribed.

I made an appointment with another psychologist to get a second opinion. This Doctor prescribed the Rorschach, or "ink blot" test. This test allows the doctor to determine if a person is mentally ill by having them look at inkblots on paper, which form various shapes. Often, doctors can even correctly diagnose the precise illness from which the subject is suffering. My test results showed the same diagnosis: Paranoid Schizophrenia.

After a few weeks and much persuasion, my therapist talked me into filling the prescription the psychiatrist had given me, and to start taking the medicine. I noticed upon the first day of taking medication that I felt extremely tired, and yet anxious. The side effects were horrendous. I had no energy. I had a terrible time enjoying my workout that very day, whereas the previous day before starting the medication, I completed my workout as I had for the past two years.

It was difficult trying to enjoy being in the presence of my reptile companion animals, "Rain" and "Drakos". I felt too anxious, too unsettled to do so. I felt like I should be constantly moving but didn't know what to do. Nothing was stimulating enough. I was anxious, but also tired. For the first few days on this medication I took three hour naps and I could not get enough sleep. Although I was sleeping about twelve hours at night, I felt like I had hardly slept. I had no energy and I simply felt awful. Throughout this time, I learned about the variety of symptoms caused by this illness. It was difficult, and sometimes impossible, to determine which were the symptoms of the illness and which were the side effects of the medicines I was taking.

Symptoms are divided into two categories: First are "negative symptoms", such as the flattening of emotions, or not enjoying activities previously enjoyed. These are called negative, because they are taken away from the personality. Second are "positive symptoms", such as auditory or visual hallucinations. They are called positive because they are added to what was the normal personality before onset of symptoms. Positive or negative in this case, has nothing to do with good or bad.

Prior to beginning this medication, I never had any feelings of lack of enjoyment, or lack of emotion. As mentioned earlier, I was always very emotional even before medications. This was why it was so difficult, (and impossible,) to determine which symptoms were caused by the illness, or the added stress of learning my diagnosis, or the medications themselves.

Over the course of the next few months, I continued to feel quite paranoid. In addition to carrying my knives with me everywhere I went, my mind would also produce random, strange fears. As mentioned earlier, I had developed a strange fear that I was living with HIV. Throughout the years following high school and into college, I was convinced that I contracted HIV from a tattoo I got when I was younger. This fear was strange, as its power and severity came and went. At one point, I got tested for HIV in an attempt to ease my mind. A negative test result temporarily eased my mind. However, around the time of diagnosis, the fear of having contracted HIV from my tattoo was returning with a vengeance—so much that I was fully convinced that I was living with HIV.

When I went out to eat, I would carry my own silverware with me. I did not want to contract HIV that I already believed I had, and furthermore, did not want to infect anyone else. I would not eat from public silverware. During a public outing to a restaurant, after my diagnosis, whether on a date, with friends, or family, there I would be trying to subtly pull my silverware from the small plastic bag I kept in my right pocket next to the combat knife, which was also clipped there!

Obviously this behavior does not make sense. Here is someone trying to avoid eating from silverware so as not to catch HIV that he already believes beyond any doubt, that he has, and also to protect others from catching it from him. Even though I understood at least the basics of the HIV virus, I therefore knew somewhere deep down that this was next to impossible to "catch" HIV from silverware, I was still deeply pained by this fear, living daily with the belief that I had HIV.

Thoughts of people who suffer from Schizophrenia and who are experiencing psychosis often do not make sense. This is unfortunate for people who suffer from this illness. Schizophrenia affects everything a person says and thinks, affecting their behavior drastically. They are often behaving from a state of complete fear, creating a deeply engrained array of odd behaviors, stemming from a fearful, and often defensive perspective.

This is why approaching mental illness with compassion, patience, kindness, support and education is so essential to recovery. It is the only way to approach mental illness. Far too often, in this utilitarian society, the opinionated theme regarding mental illness sounds like someone from the 1800's almost as though they were referring to their mule: "Pull up yer boot straps and get a goin!" "Toughen up!" Everyone knows someone who is going through some type of mental difficulty as I am describing. If people could only realize that mental illnesses are medical problems just like diabetes or cancer, and rather than shunning or judging the person suffering from it, encourage and support them in their treatment.

Occasionally, but not often, I experienced auditory hallucinations (voices). One occasion particularly stands out to me. On a particular day, I was having an especially difficult time adjusting to my new life with a mental illness, and I felt particularly anxious, frantic, afraid, but of nothing specific. I felt like my world was caving in. I was quickly losing hope. Whether my imagined opponents were the ill-intended people who I had trained to defend myself against, or whether they were demons, or my own thoughts, I wanted to be away from them. I barely avoided yelling publicly aloud, "Leave me alone!" I had been driving home and had just pulled into my parents' driveway, where I lived at the time. It was then that I stopped, to call out to God to relieve me from the state of utter anxiety, my state of such complete deflation. It was right then that I heard a snarling, vicious voice, "You should be praying for others, not yourself!"

Naturally, I found this frightening and deeply disturbing. In a sort of defeated manner, basically throwing my hands in the air, I crawled out of my truck, shut the door and moved like heavy tar toward the house while thinking, "Ironic, I only hear malicious voices when I talk to God." Needless to say, shortly after this, I stopped talking to God for a very long time.

Up until this time I had been attending school but had not held a job. The toll of the side effects of medication in addition to the symptoms of the disease proved too much. I dropped that semester of school. So, I was not working, and was not enrolled in school: "grand." However, on a positive note, this time off accounted for a lot. I was able to stay in a safe, secure environment, and just take it easy. That was exactly what I needed. Just as though someone were physically very ill, and needed time to recover, so did my mind. I accepted this, and just allowed some down time for myself, to take it easy, and gather myself.

During this time, I had no income. Although I lived at my parents' house and needed very little, I wanted enough money to care for my reptiles, as they were my only solace at the time. I had applied for supplemental disability income, and was denied twice. I talked to my disability agent and tried one last time. The agent assigned to my care requested that I be evaluated by another doctor. This time it was to determine my eligibility for supplemental income. After many questions, he came to the same conclusion: That I had Paranoid Schizophrenia, that I would probably never work, and would probably be in and out of jail, unable to live a normal life. After hearing this for the fourth time, I was sort of numbed to it. This evaluation finally proved me eligible for disability income. I was just grateful to have at least that, even with the horrible stigma attached to it. It meant that I would have a bit of money to continue to care for my reptiles, which, was my main concern at that time.

My reptiles and my plants gave me a certain peace. They gave me hope and life in a way that absolutely nothing else could. I would often sit down in my "rainforest room," sometimes crying, but always clinging to my "evergreen" plants and lizards. I know now that it was the pure, living energy, which I sensed from them that I so desperately needed. "Rain," my Chinese Water Dragon, with her emerald green skin, merely wanted to eat insects, swim in her pool, and then climb the branches to bask in the warmth of her heat lamp. Drakos, my Bearded Dragon wanted the same, and neither judged me nor pitied me as the guy with Schizophrenia. They would simply eat the crickets, and bask in their beautiful environment, which I provided so gratefully for them. Throughout the winter of 2001-2002, I did little else but sit there, watch them, feed them and water plants during the day, and then walk my dog Elvis in the evening, clinging to the "evergreen" life-force which they provided.

Chapter 2

A Small Step Forward

The warmth of spring gave me enough courage to begin looking for a job again. I had inquired about a job at a small, local pet store, where, at the time, I purchased many supplies for my reptiles. I was confident of my knowledge and skill with pets, even if I didn't feel my best mentally. The owner of the pet store, who I actually knew fairly well, offered me a job one day while I was buying supplies. I was surprised at the random offer, but I accepted. In May of 2002, when I was twenty-four, I began working part-time there. This turned out to offer additional income and was something to help occupy the void in my life. It gave me a sense of purpose—somewhat.

Although I wasn't feeling great at the time and had actually become accustomed to usually feeling quite lousy, this new job gave me some extra confidence. My knowledge of companion animals proved to be a valuable asset to this small pet store. I had vast experience and knowledge about caring for various pets. I knew I would be capable of helping others to do the same.

That fall (2002) I was also able to enroll in classes again at the university. Although I felt miserable most of the time and was actually still quite paranoid, but I decided to give it a shot.

There were days throughout that semester that I felt particularly paranoid. On these days, I expected that the worst would happen. Sometimes, I was completely fear-stricken, expecting that the tall building in which my class was held would be bombed, or that a plane would be flown into the building. (This was not quite a year after the 9/11 terrorist attacks in 2001. I was still holding onto fears about this.)

At times I would become so fearful while in that building that I would have to distract myself by becoming extremely social. Often, while in the middle of a lab, the class would be busily interacting, working on their tasks, as students normally would. I would become so nervous that I began talking to other students, joking with them, laughing with them asking them random questions in almost a manic way. This was all in an attempt to distract myself from my inner fear.

I remember the looks on several of the student's faces, and how strange I must have appeared to them. What they didn't realize was that I was trying to enjoy the moment, and help them enjoy their last moments, because I was sure that we were all going to be killed at any second. Obviously, the medications I was on were not entirely effective.

One benefit this medicine did have for me though, was that I was not as explosive or hostile, ever ready to explode into action and use the lethal martial arts skills, which I had practiced for so many years. This could have been due to the fact that the particular medicine I was taking at the time made me extremely tired. I was too tired to fight if I were attacked. In that regard, I suppose being tired was a benefit. I still believed that I would be attacked, but I had no energy to fight if I was, and no energy to practice in preparation for it, or even to feed my fear regarding it.

Fall turned to winter 2002, which slowly unfolded, and I did manage to pass my Botany course, where I had to force myself to sit through each grueling lab where I thought the building was a target of terrorism. I enrolled for the following 2003 spring semester. Confidence was slowly but surely returning, although I still suffered from both symptoms and side effects from the medication most of the time. I took the things I was trying to juggle rather slowly. I now had a part time job, enrolled and passed my courses in college, and was open to trying new things.

In March, 2003, there was one particular visit with my psychiatrist, which proved to be a "mile stone" in my progress. At this point, I was fearful enough that I was still carrying my combat knives. Before every visit with him, I would unclip the knives from each pocket and leave them in my vehicle before entering his office. I did this out of respect for his request on my first visit to never bring them again.

The medicine had calmed me down enough that I actually grew quite fond of my doctor. I no longer saw him as a creepy porn addict, but a distinguished, intelligent doctor that was truly concerned and was doing everything within his ability to help me. (Currently, I still have a deep respect and appreciation for him.)

As I sat in his office, I was able to articulate how awful I felt on this particular medication that I had been taking since my diagnosis in November 2001. I explained how, the previous semester, I thought the lab building was going to be bombed or attacked by terrorists, and how the students had looked at me so strangely as I became abnormally social at horribly awkward times, and strangely animated amidst labs. I informed him of my most recent fear: that I didn't like people walking behind me, whether I knew they were real or not, and if anyone was doing so for what I thought was too long, I would stop and pretend that I was distracted by something, and I would allow them to pass.

I explained how I still completely expected to be physically attacked where I would have to use my Martial Arts skills, but that if I had to use them, I would be too tired to do so. I also explained that I felt that the medicine made me so tired that I didn't want to practice or train for this dreaded day, and I was rarely working out anymore, as I used to so much enjoy. I explained that I had not experienced the anxiety, social awkwardness, and fears before, at least not to this severity. I explained how since beginning the medication, my behavior seemed more like depressive symptoms, and I wasn't sure anymore what was illness and what were side effects of my medicine. I explained how I really could not enjoy anything. I felt a limited range of emotion, (very different from how I was before beginning the medicine.) The only emotions I could feel were depression, guilt, and deeply held resentment, which was building. I told him how before this particular medicine, I enjoyed life much more, even though I believed I would be attacked, I at least "had fun in the meantime." In short, I felt awful. That day was March 29th of 2003. I was twenty-five.

He thought for a moment, as he was writing notes on his clipboard, and then with a look of sympathy, he mentioned the prospect of trying a new medicine. I was surprised at this, but anxious to try anything to feel even a tiny bit better than I did.

I told him that I felt very open to trying something new. I took the new prescription to have it filled that day. For two weeks, I was to taper down the previous anti-psychotic medicine. Then after this period, when it was out of my system, I was to begin the new one. I did so, and noticed an immediate difference for the better.

On this new medicine, much of my old self was back. I could think more clearly, I enjoyed more thoroughly my reptiles, walks with Elvis, and I could even converse with people on a more "typical tone." This new medicine even allowed me to do these things with fewer symptoms, and definitely with a decrease in severity of symptoms. I even started enjoying activities that I had forgotten I once enjoyed. I found my life returning. It was a blessed relief; however, I was irritated with myself for allowing myself to continue the previous medicine, which caused me to feel so awful for as long as I did.

I worked and attended my Geography class, and when the professor lectured about the distance from Sun and Earth, and how most ultraviolet rays bounce back, I thought of my Water Dragon, Rain at home, and how this related to her and her species in the wild. I noticed that my "geek-naturalist" self was on the rebound, and knew that this was a good thing as I felt more myself. I therefore thought of the new medicine as heaven-sent. I passed my geography course that May, and life was again *life*.

Throughout this period, I was eating a lot and my exercise was nearly non-existent. I gained twenty-five pounds rather quickly, and did not look like the lean, serious Martial Artist that I had been in 2001.

A Bit of a Sting

I was proud to have passed two semesters at the university, and proud to have a part time job. In my leisure time that summer, I was researching other reptiles and found a big book of reptiles that I decided I really wanted: "The Completely Illustrated Atlas of Reptiles and Amphibians for the Terrarium". I had a part-time job and supplemental disability income to pay for it. It was over eight hundred pages long, but I *so* thoroughly enjoyed immersing myself in research, learning, and reading about these creatures once again. I had plans to order the book and had been saving my money; it was about a hundred dollars.

Shortly thereafter in June of 2003, I was fired from my employment with the pet store for not following directions, and in the words of my boss, "You just don't seem to be catching on like the others." I felt terrible about this. It seemed that every time I would get a bit of confidence and start to go somewhere, it would be smashed to the ground and stomped on.

I went through with the purchase of the book. "If I can't hold a bloody job, at least I'll have lots of knowledge about reptiles, the one thing I still enjoy," I said to myself, as I submitted the shipping order to be shipped to my parents' house.

This event sparked some bitterness over my situation, although this time not outwardly hostile but rather inwardly imploding. I blamed all of this on the belief system, or religion, which I had grown up with, and on God. I believed that I was being punished for deeds throughout my life, and that God just liked to test me as His lab rat. It made no sense to me that I would get somewhere, experience some hope, and then I would fall, or rather, God would let go of me, and there I would be hitting the ground hard, and that in the long run, I was not going anywhere.

Little did I know that these years were forming a crucial foundation for me, one, which later was to provide a springboard and a solid platform for tremendous growth to occur. I did not talk to God very much in those days, and the few times that I did, I was cursing and expressing my anger. Bitterness was becoming my state in general, particularly with anything concerning religion or God. I had found it increasingly difficult to finish my martial arts workouts until I had nearly stopped them altogether. I gained more weight. I was rarely attending my martial arts classes. It seemed pointless. Sure, the new meds had given me some relief—but I was rapidly gaining weight, I still could not hold a job, and there I was spending my last one hundred dollars on an eight-hundred page reptile atlas.

Chapter 3

Try This Route to Hope

I had heard about a local support group, by the National Alliance on Mental Illness (NAMI). The support group was structured as a weekly class and was known as "B.R.I.D.G.E.S.", which stands for Building Recovery and Individual Dreams and Goals through Education and Support. I was quite open (and desperate) to trying new routes in helping me find some confidence, some hope. I decided to give it a chance. My first day of class, I was cynical and pessimistic; after a few of these weekly meetings though, this turned out to be exactly what I needed. The teachers of the course were a married couple, Rolf and Pam. They had three grown kids with Biological Brain Disorders (mental illness) and had been through many hard times with them. It has been said, "Nothing speaks louder than experience," and here, this statement was so true. They had "been through it all," and could relate to people within the group incredibly well. The two of them together were a refreshing change for me, a personality pair that suited me very nicely. Rolf was strong, yet light and humorous when it was appropriate. Pam was gentle and caring. Together, they were masters at instructing the class; their concern for each individual in the class was apparent. I felt a bond with them rather quickly, and a certain "click" with their personalities.

I took what I learned from that class, applied it and cherished it. I found it interesting and therapeutic to hear of other's experiences. Upon learning first hand that other people had been through similar experiences, many much worse than my own, I was comforted, educated, and came to thoroughly enjoy each week's class.

I came to love not only the instructors, but the other students as well. Tight bonds were formed. I attended these classes faithfully for several years. I looked forward to walking through the door of that building, smelling the air freshener that had a wonderful cloves and cinnamon aroma, reminding me of Christmas time, which I had always loved. I would bask in the warm, positive, healing energy that Rolf, Pam, and the group had to offer. It just happened that Rolf and Pam even had the same kind of dog as I did, and we compared notes and laughed about our dogs often. Even though it was a support group, it felt more like family. Some intense, difficult times were shared within the group over the years; and all those involved in these classes became very close, all uplifted together. It warmed my entire being to know that I truly was not alone. Many other people had experienced the same onslaught of difficulties. It also led me to realize that I had more to be grateful for than I had realized throughout the past few difficult months.

I would leave every class, feeling completely prepared to move forward. I would come home from each class eager to tell what I had learned with all who would listen, and how I related. I was always excited to share with others the soul food, the bonding laughs, tears and friendships that I had experienced there. It was truly a healing point in my life. I had climbed to the next step. Prior to finding these NAMI courses, I had virtually given up; having decided to live with my reptiles and plants in my parents' basement on disability income. The NAMI courses offered me time to be kinder to myself, and to focus more on the enjoyment of learning about my disorder, and even being able to laugh about some things. For me, it took away the feeling of impending doom, or of being forever scared stiff about my future.

Chapter 4

A Boost of Confidence

About the time that I decided to give up on looking for a job, I was met with a hard (but loving) knock of resistance. I had decided to live in my parents' basement with my reptiles and plants on disability income, because I couldn't hold a job, would never marry, and was not feeling any willingness to try at all. I had given up.

Both my therapist and Rolf strongly disagreed with this decision. (This was the hard but loving knock of resistance.) They insisted that I *could* work, that I had gifts, a purpose, and that I was capable of functioning normally. However, I resisted their encouragement, stating bitterly that I had been let down one too many times, and I wasn't up for being knocked flat again.

My therapist and I had a frank talk about this during one particular visit. I was angry and didn't like being told that I needed to try once more to start going somewhere with my life. To me, all I saw was another chance to get knocked on my face and stomped on. I knew my therapist had my best interest in mind, but I did not believe it was possible; I didn't believe in myself. I was done. This particular visit with my therapist is only one of two etched in my memory as unpleasant. That day, I left her office very upset; I was upset, but knew deep down that she was right. I hated that she was—it meant that I had to try once again. After my mood calmed, I was more receptive to once more allow myself to hope for a normal, happy, productive life.

Rolf was able to put me in touch with a program, which assigned to me an agent who assisted people with disabilities to obtain and hold jobs.

This job coach was great. He helped me to prepare my resume, and even drove me to apply at my places of interest. His name was Jason.

I applied at several nurseries and pet stores naturally, being my areas of expertise. At the end of March 2004, to my own dismay, I had an interview with a local hardware store. I had applied there in hopes of have a chance in their garden department where I could use my knowledge and skill with live plants.

I was actually surprised at my minimal stress level—I was barely nervous. I intended to give it my all, with high hopes, but no expectations. During the interview, I was asked about my state of unemployment, being unemployed since my termination with the pet store the previous June. I had not enrolled in classes at the university for the summer or fall semesters following my being terminated from the pet-store. My inner guidance seemed to take over however, when asked about my unemployed state. The interviewer asked what I had been doing for the past nine months. With all the confidence I could muster up, I replied, "I try to stay in shape…I work out sometimes, I have some pets that I care for…. I just… try to keep busy." This seemed to be enough for him. I knew to be clear and honest about my disorder. I told him that I was taking medication for a brain disorder.

He only asked me what would happen if I missed my medicine. "Does missing your medicine cause you to hurt yourself or anyone else?" He observed me carefully, awaiting my response.

"I never have before." I replied.

No further questions were asked.

On March 31st 2004, I was hired! I was hired as a seasonal loader in the garden department. Then I *was* nervous—I actually had succeeded! However, it was a good nervousness, it felt good. I had a job; even if it was only to be seasonal; I decided I would take it with gratitude one day at a time.

As exciting as this was for me, I was slightly worried about letting go of my disability income, which was so difficult to obtain. The words of the doctor who determined my eligibility for disability income about not being able to work, and likely living in and out of jail always rang in my head. However, I let go of this worry, and the possibility that I may again, be fired, and let down again. I attended the orientation two days later. I still had the habit of carrying my knives, and casually brought my knife into the orientation clipped to my pocket as always. When the orientation agenda covered the topic of no weapons at work, they asked if anyone had any with them. I shyly showed my one knife that I had with me. This became the perfect example to then teach the policy that no weapons were allowed at work. The instructor of the orientation informed us that knives such as mine were not allowed at the store, (company policy,) and that it was not necessary for me to bring it, as they provide their employees with box cutters.

I gave an inward sigh of relief. "Yes, a box cutter! We'll go with that!" I said to myself with a chuckle.

I began the following Monday. It was the busy season early in spring in the garden department. I found that I really excelled in this area. Between helping customers carry out heavy loads of soil and patio block, my knowledge of plants helped tremendously. Both customers and employees were always impressed with my knowledge of plants and the quality of my service. Being appreciated was so uplifting! Confidence and optimism were returning to me again.

I had a department manager, Joanne, who was so understanding and compassionate when I told her of my disorder. She was easy to talk to, and always spoke with kindness and respect. She was always willing to listen and accommodated anything I needed since I was honest from the beginning in communicating about my disorder.

Meanwhile I tried very hard to be dependable and to not ask for any special accommodations. Her kindness, understanding, and listening ear were enough. I felt supported and respected, and that was accommodating enough for me. If things got very chaotic and overly stressful for me, I found that simply stepping outside and allowing my mind to slow down worked wonders. (Symptoms of Schizophrenia are almost always worsened under high levels of stress.)

I continued with this job, remaining mostly in the Outside Garden department doing what I loved, and doing what I knew. The supervisors could see that I was skilled at what I did. Occasionally I had an especially stressful day and I would start to have symptoms. I would simply explain briefly and they would let me go home for the day, no questions asked, although this was rare. Still, they really were great to work with me when I needed it, knowing that I did the best I could. I continued to visit my therapist and psychiatrist faithfully, as well as attending the Bridges courses on Wednesday evenings. They were all happy for me that I had managed to find and hold a job. I was determined to become as well as possible.

The newer medicine was wonderful. It seemed to be the answer for me at the time. It seemed heaven-sent. I hoped it would be the one I would continue taking for my entire life. I had still experienced occasional symptoms, but they definitely seemed to be minimal. I was not entirely "cured," and I was planning to live as such, but I was okay with this; I had my new job with income, and my precious reptiles. Life was back again, and I was content with these few, simple pleasures I had thought would never again be mine.

At that point in time, while not at work I still carried my knives everywhere except work, but it was more out of habit than from feeling truly afraid. This was another benefit of the medicine, in that I didn't obsess about being attacked as I once did. I always did have a sort of "what if I do get attacked" in the back of my mind, but I didn't obsess about it. It didn't control my life.

Chapter 5
A Random, but Profound Insight

One occasion, while driving home from a check-up appointment with my psychiatrist, I was listening to a song by Dave Matthews band, "Warehouse". I was appreciating the sound of the music, which, to me, had a sort of "island" sound. I began to ponder the lyrics, and wondered what they meant. I experienced randomness of thought. My thoughts turned to Mahatma Gandhi, who I had always admired, in learning about him in school, but about whom I knew very little. With the island-like music playing, I also began to randomly think of people from the Pacific Islands. I believe my perception of these people stems from an experience I had as a small child, approximately six years of age, when a man of this nationality had seen me crash on my bike. He ran over to me, effortlessly scooping me up from the asphalt, and then carried me some distance home to my parents' house as my scraped knees and elbows bled. I had not reflected on this experience before this moment in the car. With my mind still flowing, the "theme" seemed to be Mahatma Gandhi combined with the fine people of the Pacific Islands. Sound random? That's because it was! As I thought about these people, I admired how gentle and kind those whom I had known from this area of the world were, beginning with the one who rescued me as a kid.

My mind darted back to Mahatma Gandhi with positive, loving thoughts of complete and utter respect. At this time, a sudden thought crossed my mind, almost voice-like, "Gandhi would not carry knives."

I understood this very simple, but profound thought in that moment. Still, I seemed to be in a sort of trance, allowing my thoughts to flow as I pondered the gentle people of the Pacific islands and the lyrics of Dave

Matthews. As I enjoyed this reverie, I felt in tune, calm, balanced, and receptive, like a radio that was full of static when it finally locks into a strong, clear signal. As I listened to the beauty of the song, and thought upon the great people, I began to cry... intensely. I found myself sobbing once again while driving home. This was a deeply spiritual experience; it was a very pivotal one. It was then and there that I decided to give up carrying my knives altogether. This I did. I never carried them again. I put them away, as well as my guns. Out of sight, out of mind.

Things were going well; I was seeing life as "ay-ok" again. I was working full- time with virtually no bills due to the fact that I still lived in my parents' basement. This left me with some disposable income. I had acquired quite the interesting collection of reptiles, tropical plants, and even some amphibians. My fascination with the natural world, particularly exotics, was a growing passion. I was never satisfied with what I had. I always wanted more. (Later, I was to realize the amount of suffering I brought upon myself with this sort of thinking, but of course, I didn't know it at the time.)

I continued to put the majority of my focus toward these wonders of nature; although my life was filling up with them fast, I loved them. My reptiles were my everything! It was my favorite activity to be at home in the various "reptile rooms" watching them in as close to a natural habitat as I could possibly provide. This often included live plants, pools, special spectrum lamps, heat lamps, room sized habitats, and even some with waterfalls. I found them therapeutic, and decided that I needed them as much as they needed me. It was like having my own little square of rain forest in my room. This brought me great joy. Giving my time and energy to these living beings proved to be very calming for my senses. These "freaks of nature" as many people would believe them to be, did something for me that absolutely no one, nor anything else on Earth could do. I felt completely nourished by them.

During the course of those few years, I had dated off and on. I had met one young woman who did not run the other way when I told her of my diagnosis. That was my first green light. We became friends. We were able to laugh freely and talk easily. This was all good news for me. She understood my mental illness, and liked my animal companion reptiles, even my big, slobbery dog, Elvis. What more could I ask for?

I asked Kelli to marry me at the July 4th fireworks, just before the show began. I had arranged for the host of the fireworks show to make the announcement, and I got down on one knee in front of all of those people—something I didn't think I would ever do. I was a small miracle. I had just spent several years being afraid, paranoid, and quite wary of people. But despite my nerves and my past demons, there I was proposing to my girlfriend, as it was publicly announced in front of thousands of people. I even amazed myself as I carried out this feat, like a spectator cheering on his favorite player. I was quite touched at how people (even total strangers at that) cheered and formulated warmth and mutual good will together on my behalf. I seemed to step out of the chapter of so strongly distrusting people, to accepting the embrace of my fellow humans.

Kelli said yes. We were married on October 22nd, 2005.

We didn't have much money at the time, so we lived in the downstairs, mother-in-law apartment in the basement of my parents' house. We simply took over where I had lived my entire life.

Before we were married, I had shared with her my feelings on not wanting to have any children. I told her several of my reasons for this. I explained to her that I believed that my gifts were something more along the lines of helping animals and plants, helping people to understand the importance of them; a sort of botanist-naturalist- spiritualist path. I explained that I wasn't certain how, what, when, or where I was to fulfill that purpose yet. She indicated that she was okay with that. This brought me renewed hope and joy, believing that a somewhat "normal" life no longer seemed so far out of the question, and no longer seemed like too much to ask. We had fun times, always felt a sense of security aside from feeling over-worked and having no extra money. In autumn, just before we were married, I had taken her to a local reptile expo/show. I purchased a tiny baby Box Tortoise for her, which she had said she always wanted. She was thrilled with him! We watched him eat together daily; she seemed just as excited as I was. It felt like a bond developing between us, a similar interest.

One January day in 2006, we discovered that our tortoise had swollen eyes. We took him to a local reptile veterinarian. The topic of reptiles as companions naturally came up with the assisting technician, who I definitely noticed as I mentioned a few of my own reptiles.

As we decided among various treatment options available for the tortoise, she mentioned a few of her own reptiles, which she cared for at home. I was impressed with all of her reptiles and knowledge of them. It was amazing to hear someone who knew as much or more about them as me!

The day had begun with Kelli acting particularly irritable which I didn't understand, but did not dwell on it. She became increasingly agitated as I casually conversed with the technician about reptiles, and all the different things we had tried in caring for our own. The Veterinarian administered the necessary antibiotics and medication, and over the next few weeks our tortoise friend became much better after several follow-up doses which Kelli administered. It was a relief for both of us to watch his health return.

Kelli and I had a great Halloween and Thanksgiving together. We experienced romance right along with the festivities of the holidays as a newlywed couple. For Christmas, I purchased a leopard gecko for her, which she had told me she really wanted. We slept Christmas Eve night on an air mattress that we inflated on the floor beneath the Christmas tree. I felt so fortunate; there I was a newlywed—something that, considering the last three years, I had stopped believing possible. We laughed, joked and reminisced—all part of the Christmas magic. If only two years prior, amidst my dark times of diagnosis, I could have taken a peek into this moment of my future, it would have been easy to continue!

I began to become more and more comfortable with my new life married to Kelli. In the cold of winter, my views of life were comfy, cozy and grateful; a blessed, welcome relief. With inner-warmth, life, gratitude, and hope graciously returning, like "feeling" once again returning to the cold, numb hands as they regained warmth outstretched to the fire, I realized that these feelings were long overdue. Life once again seemed ay-okay, something that I could get used to and cozy up to quite nicely. There I was living a long lost dream, now found. Christmas Eve, into Christmas Day, into New Year's celebrations, all part of a well celebrated new life, living the dream of the present, as learned from the past, and looking to the future.

My cozy feeling of arrival, optimism, and hope was crowned with an equally romantic Valentine's Day. I had everything I wanted in life; life was good. I had finally arrived. My theme: A sigh of relief and something of an utterance upwards, "Thank you."

Chapter 6

Darkness Falls

Only a few days after Valentine's Day, Kelli announced that she was leaving me. She said it was because I did not want children, and she definitely did, but I felt it was more than that. I tried for days to talk with her and work things out, although wasn't entirely sure what we were working out.

"What's wrong? What's going on?" I would ask her for an explanation, *any* reason for her abrupt decision to leave me. This was so random! I definitely wanted to make it work out.

"Somehow we can do this. We can work it out." I said.

She absolutely refused. Her mind was made up. It seemed like this time, something inside of *her* snapped and everything I would say to persuade her to stay only made it worse, steeling her resolve to leave. There was much confusion, trauma, heartache, many tears, (at least on my end,) and once again, my confidence was shattered. It felt like such a slap in the face, such a stab in the back. One moment my wife and I are in love, things are going well after the holidays; life was good…wasn't it?

"What the hell is this? I yelled to myself, to God, and to anyone really, who would listen. I blamed everyone and everything, especially myself. I also blamed God. I decided that I hated everything about anything that resembled God and holiness. I became extremely angry, inwardly hateful, and bitter. The last time I saw her, at the end of February 2006, I walked with her to her car, for what I knew was to be for the last time.

She was angered to the point of silence, refusing to say anything at all. After all, what more was there to say? We were both upset by the nastiness of the previous two weeks, and the raw pain and trauma from the eighty mile per hour head-on collision with a concrete wall, which was what her abrupt decision felt like. I gave her a hug good-bye anyway. Almost nothing was said; as I watched her get into her car, scarcely able to focus through my tears, I couldn't help but notice a crow, which flew right over our heads. It struck me, and although I didn't give it much thought at the time, I never forgot it. I always took it as an omen. I've read that in some Native American spiritual traditions, crows represent the natural cycle of life, death and rebirth. At that time, I only saw death.

I decided to take three weeks of personal leave work from the hardware store for a personal crisis. The trauma of Kelli suddenly leaving was just too much. Undergoing much added stress, and harsh, strenuous emotions, I felt as though I was slipping into the realms of mental illness again. I was feeling a relapse of many of my previous symptoms. I experienced a wide array of inner turmoil, emotions, which ranged from deeply buried anger, with its cousin, acidic bitterness, and accompanying relatives, spite, jealousy and hatred. These were my genuine feelings after such an abrupt loss, but these intense emotions brought back various symptoms of my disorder. In dwelling so much upon pain, and negativity, it was next to impossible to focus on the customers at work. I was a mess. I simply needed to take some time to heal.

The next few months were to be some of the darkest times of my life. I had been blaming God for everything that had gone wrong, and "for giving me this illness in the first place, which was the source of all my problems." I gained a lot more weight over this period. From my lean 126 pounds as a vegetarian martial artist, I was now at least forty pounds heavier. I was generally unhappy.

Still, I tried to remain open and tried to be guided by the universe, even though this more often than not included some combination of inward screaming, yelling and cursing this very universe. I went from spiritual, uplifting types of music, as I mentioned earlier, to dark, heavy music of hatred and anger. The darkness of mood in the music and lyrics were ironically soothing to me, for they illustrated exactly how I felt inside; I was a spinning, toxic brew of hateful anger. After all, it felt as though what little I did have going for me and which I had worked so incredibly hard for, had just caved in, and all I had left was a huge pile of debris, dead weight, rubble from my previous life, a life that was actually starting to go somewhere. I decided that I could not even see clearly to sift through, all this debris, and really didn't even care to. "If God sees me as an experimental voodoo doll, or lab specimen, testing how the universe works, or a testing the limits of what people can endure, then that God hates me; so therefore, I hate God."

The spring of that year did not feel like spring at all. Although life was teeming around me, and I was surrounded by warmth, and light, I felt dark, cold, and dead inside. I had to try to adjust to being a divorcee. I never thought this would be a word in my vocabulary, but there it was. Being that we were only married four months, I was not even adjusted to married life before having to adjust to divorced life. It was a cold, hard, magnified whiplash at its worst; and for one last, hard kick while I was already well below zero, I still had one payment left on her wedding ring.

Chapter 7

Wait Until the Smoke Clears

I did receive words of encouragement from my therapist Carol, and Pam and Rolf, the instructors at Bridges. They explained to me in their wise way, that everything happens for a reason. They told me stories of their son, who went through the same thing. "The sun shines once again."

I chuckled, *choosing* to believe his words, but any hint of hope or belief immediately dissipated with my chuckle. I chose to close myself off from hoping and striving, or longing for one more "if only, what if," that would never come. I could not risk this devastation ever again. This was it.

Throughout spring and summer, I dated off and on more for casual fun and distraction than actually hoping for anything more. I met a few young women and had fun times with them. I mostly tried to just enjoy those moments while they lasted and not become too hopeful for any sustained happiness. It seemed that fun in the moment was what I needed and preferred at the time. One to three fun dates each seemed to be the natural cycle we went through, we were in different phases, experiencing different seasons, and that was fine.

In mid-summer, I didn't do much except work and acquire more reptile companions. This seemed to be the one thing that helped me to keep my sanity, and from completely folding. The anticipation of opening a new package from UPS which contained an exotic, rare reptile that I had searched for diligently, and finally found, numbed all my pain even if temporarily. This seemed almost like an addiction, or at least an intense obsession.

I had acquired quite the collection. They were well cared for and loved. I had my parents' basement filled entirely with large enclosures full of various species of lizards, snakes and a few frogs, always with diverse native tropical plants.

I figured that being divorced, no one would want to marry me again. I planned on remaining single and living in my parents' basement for the remainder of my life. This indeed painted a bleak picture for me, but I wanted to make the most of it, figuring that it was the only option I had.

This was my reason for acquiring anything and everything I ever wanted, mostly reptiles. This was my way of splurging. I thought nothing of searching, hours at a time online, for the species I wanted. If it was rather pricey, I simply saved my money. After all, what else did I have to spend money on?

One thing I did have going for me, in spite of my extreme negativity at the time, was that I did seem quite mentally stable. I did not seem to be bothered by many symptoms as I had in the recent past. I wasn't symptom free, but mostly stable, taking my medicine and doing rather well, not really happy, but not really miserable either.

As summer turned to fall, I could feel the weight of this dark year slowly sinking in like a wound that appears to heal and later reveals an abscess deep under the skin. I had not yet figured out a way to shake the fact that my "eternal companion", my soul mate, had left me so suddenly, unexpected, abruptly, at random.

Interestingly now in hindsight, I can scarcely remember anything about that entire year. I can usually remember highlights of years, holidays, Halloween of this year, or Thanksgiving of that year; but that was not the case in 2006. Things were as dark as dark could be. I was in a complete daze with scales over my eyes, like a snake preparing to shed its skin. What would my new skin be? I was about to find out.

Chapter 8

Let There Be Light

At the end of November 2006, for the first time in nearly an entire year, I finally felt well enough to do something beyond the routine of working, watering plants, and hanging out with reptiles.

My mind experienced a nagging to take my Chinese Water Dragon, "China Doll," (named after a Chinese plant,) who seemed ill, to the vet. I had denied this inner nagging for months, in a state of denial, hoping that he was fine. At this point, I finally decided to do something about it, finally having the clear state of mind and the emotional energy. He seemed sickly enough, that I thought I was going to have to say my goodbyes to him.

I had not had much experience with sick reptiles; mine were well cared for and frankly, rarely became sick. This was new to me. I called the reptile vet to whom Kelli and I had taken our box tortoise previously.

I mentioned to the voice on the phone that I was looking at the possibility of saying goodbye to my Water Dragon. I was inquiring about financial options and other details. I told her that I would make a decision and get back with her.

"Should I ask for you when I call back?" I asked.

"That would be fine, just ask for SynDee."

I tried to put a face to the name, but couldn't quite place it. After considering my options for a few days, I made the appointment for Dec. 1st, 2006. I took China Doll into the vet office, prepared to say goodbye. I asked for SynDee, with whom I had spoken to on the phone. The receptionist misunderstood and thought I asked for "Shaylee." She pointed to Shaylee, who turned around and greeted me.

"Hi"....long pause as she blankly looked at me, "I have an appointment for my Water Dragon, I believe it was SynDee I talked to."

"Oh, I'm Shaylee. Have a seat and I'll get SynDee for you." She said, handing me some paper work to begin.

I was taken to an exam room to see the reptile veterinarian, the same doctor who saw the tortoise. He was concerned about my Water Dragon after examining him closely. I told him that I sensed he was in pain and I could see that his eyes were bothering him. I didn't believe there was anything that I could do for him.

He was silent as he concentrated heavily on China Doll's swollen eyes. He finally said, speaking in a sympathetic tone as he looked at the lizard: "I hate to just give up on ya." I perceived that he was *really* talking to me. I was silent, waiting for him to offer an alternative.

"Let me go find my tech, who *loves* reptiles, and see if she has anything she wants to do."

"Ok". I replied, relieved at the thought of a possible alternative for him. I waited for a few minutes, which seemed like a long time.

In the back of my mind, there was a lingering disappointment that SynDee, the technician who was so helpful, understanding and patient on the phone, was not the one to help me with China Doll. I was puzzled as to why I didn't get to talk to her about him, while at the office, when she was clearly so helpful on the phone. I brushed it off, reminding myself of how busy they were.

The doctor finally returned with the technician who I immediately recognized as the one who had helped with Kelli's tortoise. She was the one who had, that same day, told me of her Iguana and turtles that she cared for. "This is SynDee." The doctor casually introduced her to me.

"Ah, she *is* still here." I had wondered if she was no longer employed there. I was pleased, not only was she the one who was so helpful on the phone in the first place, but she was also the one who I found so captivating as she told me of her reptiles during that first visit with Kelli and the tortoise.

"Hi, I remember talking to you on the phone about him." I said, glad to see her again. She returned the greeting with a smile as she began to closely study China Doll.

During the silence, while we all observed him closely, I asked SynDee:

"How is your turtle?" With a puzzled expression, she said that her turtles were doing well.

I felt accepting energy from her that I found intriguing and peculiar. She seemed to respond to my slightly reckless and playful manner in a positive way. She was definitely interesting. With a serious, yet somewhat flirtatious tone, I said, "You should come see some of my reptiles. I have some exotic ones…….."

(Long pause.)…."I love reptiles," she said shyly, flattered, but not sure how to respond.

I said nothing more, as we were still focused on China Doll.

After much discussion, the doctor left the room, saying that he would be back while we decided. It was silent for a bit as we thought about our options for my Water Dragon.

"Is he too much for you, or….?" she asked warmly.

I could not help but notice the way she was looking at me as I began to explain. She was looking at me with a sort of softened expression. I hadn't seen this from anyone in a very long time. I felt the way it feels after a long winter when for the first time of the season, one experiences the warmth of the sunshine on their face. I was experiencing acceptance again, from someone else, a woman, and something stirred within me.

"I just sense that he is in pain. I have difficulty with that." I said with sincere calmness. I went on to explain that I give him his supplements and vitamins, and change his water daily, and that I could not figure out why he was falling ill. "His brother, who he shared enclosures with during his younger days, bullied him a lot. I wonder if that has anything to do with it?" I looked at her, awaiting her opinion.

Several moments passed as she observed China Doll. After a thoughtful silence, she tentatively mentioned that she would be able to take on guardianship of him. She mentioned it shyly enough that it seemed as though she expected that I would shatter this idea into tiny pieces.

I was actually very grateful at the idea. I saw this as someone who could nurse him back to health. Over a few minutes of discussion, I decided to let her become China Doll's new guardian. I signed some adoption papers as I volunteered a lot of knowledge on how to care for him. I was proud of my knowledge of this lizard species. I had read and researched a great deal about them.

I volunteered to write down some care notes for her as I explained the details of what I was writing down. "I hope you can read my writing." I joked; expecting her to say that my writing was fine.

Then, in her patented, humorous yet matter-of-fact professional manner, "I hope so too."

This made me chuckle. I found that her "matter-of-fact" style put me at ease, made me laugh, mystified me, and yet, kept me stretching slightly beyond my comfort zone, all at the same time. I wasn't sure if she remembered me or not; I definitely remembered her. I informed her that he was a tropical species, and as with her Iguana, needed high humidity and warm temperatures, and to change the water dish often.

"If you should change your mind or anything, you can call me." She said, as she wrote her phone number on the receipt.

I gave her my phone number as well, allowing her to call with any questions. "Maybe we could go to Petsmart and I'll show you everything you need." I said, trying *not* to appear flirtatious again.

"Sure, we could do that." Was there a hint of enthusiasm inflected in her voice? I chose to believe so.

I handed her China Doll. "Take good care of him... I know you will," I told her with a smile. I was definitely relieved that he was going to be okay. I knew she would be great for him.

I was inexplicably overcome from the emotional 180—I had just gone from thinking I was saying good-bye forever to China Doll, to realizing that he would live and be loved in the care of an expert. On top of that, there was the undeniable connection between SynDee and myself; I was overwhelmed by her instant trust shown, and acceptance toward me. I reacted out of pure, raw emotion, and I thank God daily that she didn't call the sheriff to haul me off for what I did next.

"I can't thank you enough," I said as I opened my arms and gave her a big hug. I was so relieved that China Doll was going to be okay; I simply had to express this.

"Oh... ok." She said, stiff and surprised.

I left the office so relieved for China Doll, and grateful to the technician who took him, but I had a lot to process! I had just experienced talking at length with the technician who not only had talked to me about my Water Dragon, but who had also been there when Kelli was with me last. She had just rescued China Doll, and I insisted on giving her a hug for doing so! I had to admit to myself that I quite liked something about SynDee.

On the way home, suddenly I thought: "Oh no! If she does remember me, she'll think I'm still married! No wonder it was weird when I invited her to see my reptiles." As soon as I walked in the door, I called the vet office with a brilliant plan. I could let her know I wasn't married any longer, and not even make it look like flirting.

"Can I speak to SynDee please?" I said to the receptionist in a hurried fashion, heart pounding.

"Hi SynDee, this is Owen, I was just there about China Doll. Would you be able to do me a favor? I noticed that Kelli's name is still on my account, but I am not with her anymore. I had asked for it to be removed awhile back, but it didn't happen. Could you remove her name for me?"

"Sure. Is there anyone else you would like me to put on the account?" she asked.

My expression must have beamed with the utterance of one word, "Nope! Thanks again, and I'll see you later," I said.

We hung up and I thought to myself, "Wow, if that doesn't give her a green light, I don't know what will! I don't think I could be any more obvious."

Shortly thereafter, I called my sister to chat. I was excited to tell her about my relief of not having to say goodbye to my Water Dragon. There was the added bonus flirtation with SynDee, but I was still guarded enough at that time that I barely mentioned it. Although the talking with SynDee had definitely begun to warm the coldness within me regarding romantic relationships, it was fun in the moment, but I was still determined not to get my hopes up. No hopes, and certainly no expectations; this was the safest policy in those days.

It was shortly thereafter that I met SynDee at Petsmart to help her find the supplies that she needed for her new Water Dragon. I arrived at the designated time and was looking at the reptiles while waiting for her. I had passed by a traffic accident on the way, and assumed that she would be late. In fact, she was so late, that I began to worry that she may have forgotten, or decided to not show.

Finally she came in the doors, looking stressed. I was relieved to see that she had shown up. She told me of the accident, and how it took her a long time to get there. As we browsed the reptile section, I was explaining to her what she would need and the purpose for each item, which I was essentially throwing into her cart. I was ever aware of how she was looking at me. At some point, I became aware that I was returning her soft gaze.

"I hope you don't mind that I renamed him Mushu," she said, almost apologetically.

I chuckled. "No, that's fine, he's yours now."

When we had finished shopping, and were ready to check out, the cashier who was watching us closely was friendly, talking to us about her own animals. We exited the store and I found myself in a situation where I knew that it was "now or never."

With the timing a bit clumsy, I blurted out, "We should go do something sometime," trying to sound as casual as I possibly could. I had learned long before that there was no such thing as casually asking a woman out any longer, especially this one. There was always such emotional risk when asking someone out, but I did it. I mostly expected her to reject me, and politely decline.

I was surprised, and even bit giddy inside as I heard her response, "Sure."

We briefly talked about our schedules, and then I told her I would call her shortly and we would go to dinner. She thanked me for the help with her new Water Dragon, Mushu, and we went our separate ways for the evening.

I called her a few days later and invited her to dinner. We arranged to go to a local Chinese restaurant that same evening. As we took our seats, I noticed that she was on guard but attentive. My being nervous seemed to cause me to tell her some details of where I was in my life, almost without thought, perhaps only knowing to be honest and direct. I began telling her the gist of my divorce. I felt it necessary to include at least the basics of my divorce, as it was a question in her mind, no doubt.

She mostly gave me attentive nods. She could see that I was nervous, but was respectful, and still guarded. This felt good, healthy, and honest, it felt right. In the coming days, we met as often as we could, and we talked on the phone the days we weren't able to meet in person. Was I getting involved with someone again? I couldn't really believe it! I was on cloud nine, as I welcomed this unexpected bonus in my life. I felt alive, and the cold darkness that had overtaken me since Kelli's leaving was brightly illuminated despite my attempts at caution and skepticism. The light overtook me and sparks turned into a flame rather quickly.

One particular evening, I was watching A Beautiful Mind with my mom and sister. This movie had become a sort of "flag ship" to me, as it perfectly reflected what I had experienced, and it helped others to understand what I could not myself express. The movie is about John Nash, a brilliant mathematician, who happened to have the same condition that I did—Schizophrenia. Nash's character was played brilliantly by Russell Crowe. I would pause the movie to explain details about the action in the movie, and the symptoms he would have been experiencing, to offer my personal interpretation of the scene. After all, I had lived it. I was quite surprised by my own knowledge about my disorder!

SynDee called in the middle of the movie. We talked for a bit. I told her of the movie I was watching. "Oh, I love that movie, I saw it six times in the theater!" She said, to my astonishment. This intrigued me, but caused me dread all at once. It also sparked some courage, knowing that I would need to tell her soon, about my mental illness. I thought it only fair to give her early warning to ditch me if she was going to do it. I knew sooner was better than later, but how I dreaded telling her!

Throughout the course of a few weeks, she seemed to be okay with my divorce and that I didn't want children. I was preparing my detailed wording of what I would say. I took some time in gathering my courage and thoughts.

We would often watch movies together in my parents' basement and talk and laugh. I showed her my reptiles many times; all the details of each, their care requirements, and she had also shown me her reptiles. I guess you could say it was serious when we introduced each other to "our children"! During one of our talks, we both agreed that we wanted to be exclusive. Everything was going so well, I knew I had to tell her….soon.

On our way to lunch one December day, I knew the moment was right. I had to tell her then. I knew I had one thing going for me—that she was safely in my car so she couldn't run away. We were stopped at a red light, and as soon as it turned green, I began to accelerate, turning left at the intersection. I knew this was my moment.

With rapid breathing, a pounding heart, and shaky speech, it seemed as if I was going to blow it before I even said anything. I thought, "This could be the end of it, before it really even begins." I didn't want to scare her away, but I *had* to tell her.

"Uh, I have something to tell you, now that we're exclusive." I looked over at her with a nervous smile. She was silent, as she looked at me, my nervousness was affecting her, but she waited for me to continue. Her body language was climbing the passenger door of my truck. I could tell she was ever prepared to jump out of the moving vehicle, should I say the wrong thing! My nervousness quadrupled. I knew I had to say it directly, briefly, without stalling.

".......uh......In 2001 I was diagnosed with a biological brain disorder known as Schizophrenia...."

In the back of my mind, I thought, "I can't believe I'm telling her this!" But I went on, trying to be nonchalant and casual, once again, toning down the tension.

"But I'm on the best medication there is available and I'm pretty much normal. I can hold a job."

"Huh... okay." She said, in what seemed to be an attempt to process the huge bit of information I had just revealed about myself. She seemed okay, but I wasn't sure.

For the next five minutes, in attempt to reassure her, I elaborated about the illness, and actually how I was quite "normal" for someone experiencing this disorder. She didn't say a lot. As we sat down to lunch, I said one last thing before I decided to shut up. "I would not be able to hide it if I were completely ill." I told her trying to show my honesty. I knew she simply needed to absorb all of it; I said no more.

A few days later, she was still around. It was a go! She wasn't freaking out. We dated all through that winter. (Christmas and New Year's were great.) Into the spring we dated and into the summer.

We had great times, as we got to know each other. We knew we would get married; we had only to decide a date.

On the Sixteenth of August, 2007, I asked SynDee to marry me. We went for a walk in a nearby canyon. When we were completely alone, with only the tranquil, trickling stream, as we sat on a log, I showed her the ring, and asked her to marry me. She answered with a hug. I knew this was yes.

Our engagement was well celebrated, and amidst all the wedding plans, we managed to spend quality time together. It seemed like our engagement in the summer, quickly turned to early spring.

We were married on March 8, 2008, when I was 31. We were both nervously excited. We find it fun to reminisce and look back on our meeting story, which seemed "straight out of a movie. Many of my co-workers liked to hear the story, and tell it to their buddies.

SynDee's co-workers sometimes made playful comments about her marrying a client of the hospital. The story is indeed, very unique. The way she and I met, and continued dating, and into marriage. It was interesting to note to others as we told the story as requested, or when asked of details, that SynDee didn't immediately recognize me as I did her, when I brought my Water Dragon to her office. She didn't recognize "the married man who had been there with the baby tortoise, but is now here with his Water Dragon." It took her being to dinner with her family after the appointment with my Water Dragon to put things together, after nearly an entire year had passed.

We sometimes reminisce about the cashier at Petsmart who served us, that first outing, buying supplies for Mushu. That same cashier is still there, and helps us often as we buy our supplies for our companion animals. (It is interesting to look back on these details.)

I find it interesting how it all came together to work out in the end. There I was at a stage where I had completely given up being down, and deflated after being slapped with a divorce, only four-months after marriage.

Then, out of the blue, when I was not even looking, I meet a young woman (through my wife at the time, Kelli.) We fall in love, and were married.

Chapter 9

This Wild Ride Isn't Over Yet

SynDee and I rented our first apartment. It was the first time for both of us being out on our own, and it brought new adventures, and new paths of learning. This apartment was very close to both of our work places and was a great starter.

Unfortunately, I was starting to experience the return of some symptoms that summer, July of 2008. I was nearly 170 pounds, close to my heaviest weight at this point. My cholesterol was quite high and I wasn't sleeping well at night. I was experiencing a general feeling of "un-wellness".

My doctor had prescribed various mood stabilizers, which I had tried with little improvement. In fact, they seemed to make my moods worse. I agreed to try them for a time however, realizing that I wanted to feel much better than I did.

One particular afternoon, during SynDee's lunch break home from work, I was feeling particularly off. She was eating her lunch, and I could not speak. I felt too sad; about what, I wasn't even sure, but I could not engage in conversation. I was not really able to listen, and/or respond to anything she would say, so we both sat at the table in silence. I simply had nothing to say, not to anyone. I was on the verge of bursting into tears, for no apparent reason, except thick sadness. SynDee noticed that I didn't seem myself, and that I didn't want to talk. I tried to explain in as few words as I possibly could that I felt a heavy sadness, and was not sure why. She looked concerned, but naturally, didn't know what to say or do.

I felt even worse knowing that I really had a lot going for me at the time. I had a beautiful, new wife. We had just rented our first apartment. I had many companion reptiles who I adored, many houseplants, and a place to call home, a decent job, a loving, supportive family, good doctors who were doing everything within their realm of knowledge to help me. None of this made me feel better. Nothing could have outweighed the depth of despair that I felt throughout that time.

I somehow continued on through this time, although with increasing thoughts of suicide. This became a vicious cycle—I would think of suicide and then feel guilty for thinking along those lines, knowing how much I had going for me, and also, knowing how devastating this would be to my loved ones, especially to SynDee. This only increased my sadness, wanting even more to end my own life. There were periods that I felt okay, and these thoughts came and went, but over time, I couldn't shake that overall sad-heavy feeling. I felt awful; medicine, sadness, guilt, and heaviness were overtaking me.

This continued through the remainder of 2008. I virtually dreaded each new day of every day of my life into 2009. Much of the year 2008 and some of 2009, seems like a blur to me. I only have a handful of memories.

SynDee and I were able to buy our first house in February 2009. This was an adventure. The details seemed to flow like a mountain stream, especially considering that we weren't even looking to buy a house at the time. I stumbled into an old acquaintance of mine who was a real estate agent. Everything came together in a matter of weeks, and it seemed as though we just clicked our heels and there we were in our new house a few miles north, in the city. This was great. It was a new chapter for us, a fresh start.

Only a few weeks later, my mood experienced another dip. I felt in a rut again. It made no sense to me; I could not place it. I had so much going for me, a new house! However, I was increasingly feeling like I was drowning in tar—thick, black, sticky junk, from which I could not escape. Since I could not trace it, this felt even more like a trap, a prison. This drove me nuts! I just wanted to fix it and feel better. I was prepared to do *anything* to escape. The increasing feeling of deflated, heavy moods was just too much. Whether drowning in sticky, black tar, or feeling as if I were drowning in some deep, dark, unknown cave waters, it was too much. It seemed like the unknown, depthless waters, vast nothingness, were all I knew.

I believed there was no escape. I believed the only options I had, was to live the rest of my life feeling this way, or die, and hopefully escape in death. I thought, "the afterlife has *got to* offer something better than this. If it does not, and there is nothing… fine, *nothing* will be better than how I feel right now."

Death was sounding more and more hopeful, and was quickly becoming a possibility, so much so that I had developed a detailed plan on every final detail of how, where, when I would take my own life. By April of 2009, I had formulated this plan completely, with every detail in order, (as much as that can possibly be,) for the taking of my own life. I simply could not live in this pitch-black cave water, or sticky, thick tar. It was too much.

My mood of thick sadness and severe depression was far more severe than the early days of my diagnosis, while so delusional and afraid. Those fearful, delusional days, ironically, seemed heavenly to return to in comparison to how I was feeling in April of 2009. If only I'd had a way to do so.

I had set a date for the following June, that if I weren't feeling better at that time, I would go through with my suicide. I wrote on the back of a receipt, to remember to put in my diary later, April 23rd, 2009: "I think of all the reasons why I should not kill myself and there are many, but then I just feel worse and want to do it even more, because I see no way out of this misery that I feel."

I have a clear memory in mind of my darkest moment that year: I was at work at the hardware store (of all places to be when one is this low), on top of a ladder, stocking freight. I was already crying, but doing my best not to break down into uncontrolled sobbing. I was grateful that no customers were around, as it was still early in the morning. The depth of the misery, which I was feeling hit me at that moment; I finally understood how drastic it was, in that I no longer wanted to live, if life meant living like that. I was absolutely certain and serious about this. The hard truth was that I didn't *want* to die. Neither did I want to live feeling the way I was. If this was life, my life could not continue. I saw it as my only option.

I was making plans at that moment. "I could go home early, saying I'm sick. I could find my gun. I know where the bullets are. I could end this suffering and misery right now."

Somehow, I picked myself up out of this moment, out of the emotional tar pit in which I had sunk to my chin, immobile, barely staying above the fatal point. I somehow hung in there for the day. I don't remember how I was able to do so.

A few days later, while still feeling low, but not to the point of directly suicidal, I mentioned this to my new therapist. He was able to help me reduce my intense sadness for the time being, but I knew it was an option for me any time things got bad enough. Ironically, this was a source of comfort to me. Yes indeed, it doesn't get any lower than this, when one feels hopeless enough that the thought of suicide brings them solace.

Despite the talk with my therapist, I still clung to the knowledge that I could choose to exit the oppressing emotions of pain, suffering, and misery at any junction of my life any time I found them unbearable. The knowledge that I had an escape available allowed me to continue onward. I could choose to end my life any time, and that was definitely still my plan for the following June. It was April, and I had set a date for my suicide for June 29th. I did so in what was something like a prayer, one that I scarcely had energy to utter, but it went something like this, "Okay, if you're there, you know how serious I am; either I feel better, or I *will* shoot myself on June 29th."

Chapter 10

Time for Real Change, Can it be True?

Amazingly, over the next few days, my mood elevated. It was at least tolerable, although this time of my life is mostly blur—I can remember almost nothing. My mood had become stable enough to where I was not immediately suicidal. I noticed June 29th approaching. However, I was well occupied and distracted researching a topic that greatly interested me. June 29th came and went. Little did I know that the elevation in my mood was only the first part of my answered prayer.

I was searching for books about diet, and its connection to both our health and the Earth. This topic had very recently intrigued me. The book I had decided to buy was Diet for a New America, by John Robbins. The decision to search out this book turned out to be the second part answer to my prayer that day. Oh, was I in for change!

Diet for a New America offered compelling evidence how a diet with little to no animal products can benefit our health and the planet as well. It was a spark of hope for me. This was the very opening of a new path; my very life was saved by it. Reading Diet for a New America started me on a series of books, from vegetarian health, to books on self-help, spirituality, simplicity, and other topics that interested me. One book or topic, led to another; they all proved to be stepping-stones on my journey of personal evolution. I was undergoing a metamorphosis, a renaissance of new ideas! The books were all gems, but I am especially grateful to Diet for a New America for "getting the ball rolling."

The prospect of possibly being able to change my health, and in doing so, also benefit the earth, was something simply irresistible to me. After I finished reading the book, I tried it. That is, in addition to my vegetarian diet, I ceased eating *all* animal products. Prior, I had relied heavily on dairy products and eggs for my vegetarian dishes.

July 31st, 2009, was my last day of being vegetarian. August 1st, 2009, I ate a completely plant based (vegan) diet. My transition was that abrupt, the only style for me! After I did so, I noticed improvement in the way I felt nearly overnight! It was absolutely astonishing. I hungered for more information along these lines.

During this time, I was almost never seen without a book. I was devouring knowledge, and I could not get enough! I read thirty-four books in fourteen months! It was like I was at a large banquet where I felt totally nourished, and where the food was so satiating that I could eat as much of what I wanted and didn't have to worry about it making me ill or fat. Hey wait, that sounds like…. Plant-based diet, oh, that's because it is! I discovered what an essential thing a plant-based diet was for me. It was an absolutely essential (and perfect) first step.

These books, these stepping-stones of knowledge, contained the right combination of facts that my mind, body, and spirit found absolutely essential. My life, at that time, *literally* depended on them. They seemed to spark something within me that said, "Let's get going!" I then *wanted* to live. I was too busy reading to think about taking my own life. Each book I found on plant-based nutrition and caring for the Earth renewed my lease on life. Book by book took me further from my dark thoughts of suicide.

I have this man to thank, John Robbins, the author of <u>Diet for a New America</u>, for being brave enough to speak out on such an unexplored topic, one most were unwilling to even approach. After all, it was <u>Diet for a New America</u> that sparked something inside of me. After reading it, then continuing to explore, and I was to never be the same.

Shortly thereafter, I began to search for doctors with extensive research and knowledge about my new diet. I wasn't surprised, but definitely was excited when I found some! In fact, these doctors of whom I speak *advocate* a plant based, or mostly plant based diet. Dr. Joel Fuhrman (Drfuhrman. com) and Dr. John McDougall (Drmcdougall.com) are the two whose work I most closely studied.

As I took notes from these DVD's, the muscles in my hands couldn't write fast enough. I found myself having to frequently pause the speech to allow my hand to catch up! It was intoxicating. Once again, my life was returning, and this time, by damn, it was here to stay! I was so excited. I loved my new outlook, my new perspective, the way I felt, the way I looked, and my new life.

I feel mountain ranges above my dark times. Those days are in the past and so distant from me now, that looking back upon them seems as if I have woken up from a really bad nightmare. At the time of this writing, I weigh 126 pounds, back to my leanness I enjoyed in 2001. This is a far cry from my heaviest, at 171 pounds in 2008. I have experienced a substantial increase in overall well-being since becoming vegan in 2009. My total cholesterol has gone from 203, on 1/23/2008, to just below 100, when it was last tested.

What has happened to me mentally and spiritually though, is the best part. I feel that I have a purpose, inspired, healthy in every way. I feel balanced. I feel how I believe we all should, and *can* feel. I feel peaceful. I feel spiritually fulfilled, in my own style, and in my own way. I find myself expressing gratitude to the universe, and a higher power once again, as I had once enjoyed long ago. This relationship has felt more real than ever before. In fact, it is now that I completely understand a lesson that a good friend taught me once, "the universe loves gratitude."

I say that I'm healthier now than I have ever been. I felt early in the year 2010 that it was going to be a big year for me. I was so right! I felt strongly that many changes would come my way, positive changes. As sung by my favorite band, 311: "It's been a wild ride; I wouldn't change a minute." I wrote in my diary that I could feel the changes coming on. I also felt that they were big, positive steps although I had no idea of their magnitude! I have achieved a lot of personal milestones, which contributed to tremendous overall growth.

Knowing what I know now, I cannot "un-know" (See the book <u>Vegan Freak</u>). I cannot go back, nor would I want to. It is all part of a collective knowledge. If I eat junk, I will feel like junk. Think about it. If every person consuming food is eating three to four or five meals a day, this adds up. Do the math; three meals a day, multiplied by 365 days a year, for 60 or more years; this adds up. As I fail in my attempt to not sound cliché and amateur here, yes, it is imperative to take into our bodies, food that is good, nutritious and wholesome; this is plants.

Chapter 11

As if That Wasn't Good Enough—
Ah, Yes Indeed, It's Fun Time!

After all the books I've read on health, nutrition, and DVD's of doctor's lectures, I've discovered that many diseases of western "affluence" can be prevented and even reversed by the plant-strong, vegan diet. Diabetes, heart disease, atherosclerosis, high cholesterol, the list could go on and on. Early in my research, I began to think, "Most diseases of various organs can be cured and reversed on this diet and lifestyle. If diet can heal the body, why can't it heal the mind? Why couldn't mental disorders such as Schizophrenia be cured also?"

In August 2010, when I was so well, but still taking prescribed medicine, I took the MMPI for the third time. It showed no mental illness. I was definitely excited, but still had a ways to go before I had the courage to ask my doctor if I could try a trial period without meds. I continued my new diet, with new outlook, and newfound joyous outlook on life. I did gather the courage to "feel out" my psychiatrist on at least the temporary cessation of my medicines. I had been bringing it up increasingly throughout my visits with him.

On December 7th, 2010, I took my medicine as I had been directed for so long. The next day, I had an appointment with my psychiatrist. The possibility of a trial period without meds was again my tentative agenda. The theme seemed to be both my doctor, and myself, questioning the wisdom in remaining on the meds if I really didn't need them.

With cautious optimism, he allowed me to leave that day without any prescription refills, a sort of "leap of faith" on his part. I left the office ecstatic, my doctor basically "scratching his head", in a sense.

The Very Condensed Version of an Entirely Different Novel

I had a blog at the time called "Schizophrenic Green Vegan", in which I posted my newfound discoveries, lifestyle, diet, optimism, and hope, and on which I also tracked my progress in regards to my disease. It was an exciting "land-marking" post that day, when I announced that I had begun a trial period with no meds. I received much feedback, congrats, and good wishes. I was elated!

It was only a few days later that SynDee and I were on our way to a Christmas party. A man backed into us with his truck, totaling SynDee's car. Sparing the unnecessary details, we sold my truck and bought a nice car, which we now share.

At this point, I began riding the bus, local train, and mostly walking to where I needed to be. Shortly after this, I cancelled my internet service thereby also discontinuing my blog, at least for the time being. It was a decision I made not only to save money which was a bit tight at the time, but also because I was closely guarding my mental health during my "trial period", and I could sense a difference in my mental well-being when I spent too much time on the computer. Being in a sense "unplugged" from computers and cars, I realized that I loved walking, loved being outside, among the birds, grass, sky, clouds, rain, snow, trees, flowers, which in early March, were just presenting their colors and fragrances. Among those that sprout early: Hyacinth, Tulip, Narcissus; to me it made little sense, to be "online" so much when being outside brought me so much joy, satisfaction, and vigor. It was at this time that I learned to really value what I now refer to as my "seasonal unplugged time."

A few weeks later (March 2011), I got out my mountain bike for the first time in over 2 years. I began riding it nearly everywhere I went—near or far. I found that I could cover much more ground in a more efficient manner, less strenuously on my body than walking the great distances, which I was covering at the time. It wasn't as easy to stop and identify flowers here or there when riding my bike, but by that time, I knew which ones were sprouting, and had memorized which families they belonged to, and how many stamens and petals were on each!

Perhaps the grand finale of the last ten years was when I was scheduled to see my psychiatrist on April 29th for one more, possibly final, evaluation. The receptionist called to inform me that the doctor was not able to attend any appointments that day. I told the receptionist that I was feeling fine, and didn't need to be seen at the time. She explained that I could call any time, should I need to be seen again; but with me doing so well, I didn't need to schedule any appointments. Another way of saying this: "Case closed!"

That moment brings to mind a fireworks display, when the crowd is taken by surprise by the grand finale, overwhelming their senses with dazzling colors in every direction, and keeps going, continues to thrill to the point where the crowd erupts into cheers. To say that I was excited, even ecstatic, is likely the understatement of the century. I spent the next fifteen minutes running around the house, singing every 311 song I could think of at the top of my lungs, jumping around, and dancing with my arms in the air. This sent our cats running beneath the couch for cover! When I went outside, I had to restrain myself from becoming a public misfit. I was absolutely ecstatic! I had fully believed and expected I would see this day; from early in my research about health and nutrition, I strongly believed I could do it. However, I didn't exactly announce this, and kept my cards close to my chest, so to speak. So when the validation of this belief came through, in the form of a closed case, it is easy to see why I released my long withheld jubilation, like the eruption of a volcano.

Currently, I do not see a psychiatrist, as I no longer need medications. As anyone, I have a regular checkup by my family physician, testing everything from cholesterol, to weight, and BMI, (Body Mass Index,) to Vitamin D blood levels. These are all within excellent ranges.

I have achieved my goal of becoming medicine free with the approval of my psychiatrist, of course. (Warning: You must consult with your doctor before attempting to cease any medications. I did the same. This is to be done only under the supervision of a doctor.)

As for me, there are two possibilities: One, my new lifestyle and diet, with a bit of exercise, and new found, deep sleep,(discussed in later chapters,) allowed my mood and my outlook to improve, which cured my Schizophrenia; or two, I never had it in the first place and my symptoms were "something else" the entire time. Neither of these possibilities is relevant to me now. The illness is in the past where it belongs. What matters now is that I am happy, healthy, pleased to read my reptile, or plant books, watch a movie with SynDee, walk in the rain, sun, snow, or wind and be grateful that I am now here. My dark times, are respectfully kept in the past, however, honored as an essential part of the journey that brought me where I am today.

Now I am happier than I have ever been. I am going somewhere in my life. I am taking care of myself and I am learning daily just what taking care of myself means. I have my beautiful wife, a place to call home with a river walk virtually in my backyard, some beloved companion animals and plants, and an income source which helps meet our needs and wants.

I have realized something golden: everything I truly *want* out of life is everything I already *have*. I have my health, my home, my wife, plants, and companion animals. I am grateful for what I do have. For me, it is enough. There are very few "extras" that I want, and if I find that I really want an "extra," I can usually find it along my journey, or perhaps have fun trying to make it.

Every once in a while I will buy an extra that I truly want, after much deciding whether I really do or not, and if I find that I do, I buy it, and I do so as a choice, with gratitude that I *can*. One of my favorite quotes is from Cody Lundin's website, of primitive living camps, "The more you know, the less you need." (codylundin.com)

In the traditional sense of the word, I am not wealthy, but I feel like the richest man on planet Earth, because every day is met with wonder, awe, gratitude for breath, for life, for abundant food and nourishing beauty. This inner wealth is within my grasp every day as a *choice*, ripe fruit on a tree waiting to be picked.

Every day I must make a choice, to pick it or not. Most days I have chosen to pick, and have been richly rewarded. On those days, there is always enough for everything that I want or need, because it is everything I already have, and I have already made the internal choice that it is enough. Thank you for reading.

--Owen Staples, botanist, naturalist

Chapter 12

High on Health

"You're high! Granted, you are high on health, but you're still high!"
-Loralyn Staples

My newfound outlook on health and happiness is that they are both a choice. The two are closely related, and therefore, have a cyclic relationship. The metaphor is a mountainous hike, a journey, and as with any journey, it is never done. It is only on to the next bend in the road, the next landscape, or the next adventure. The heights to which one aspires could be compared to mountain peaks.

I view our most valuable asset, health, from a different perspective than many. I view it from the collective lens of humanity. I prefer to see where humans have been, rather than where we are going.

The fast paced mode of our modern world is unnatural for people. It is very foreign to the human body and promotes well-being in very few ways. It is also a lifestyle that is relatively new. Our primeval inclinations and urges have hardly changed since our beginnings as humans. We still possess the same basic drives, and we are trying to feed those drives in ways we always have, but in a world that hasn't always been with us. Our modern ways are so foreign and dissonant to those primeval drives that I believe it creates both individual health problems and global problems.

Having said this, I am not recommending that we shut off every man-made device and go back to ancient ways. We are now here. We live in the present. However, I do believe that we can successfully implement some long known methods of sustainability, health, and respect for our Earth into our modern world. If we were to become more in tune with the natural rhythms of the Earth, of growth, life, death, re-birth, seasons, light cycles, this would influence our well-being as well.

I find ancient people fascinating. Sleep, activity, food, even fun time—how were these needs met in past times? I believe these people possessed a tremendous amount of respect, reverence for the Earth and all creation, including for the individual. Health and respect for their home—viewed by them as one and the same, and not separate. Taking care of their home was their priority as second nature, and in doing so, their health prospered.

Consider the ancient Greeks, Romans, ancient people of the British Isles, Native Americans, Australian Aborigines, Chinese, ancient peoples of India—not, only did each have a unique contribution to our world, old and new, but each had become true masters of the "lessons of their own land", the requirements and limitations of each land that were unique and particular to that region. These lessons of the land were respected, honored. These people knew that this helped to ensure that there was always enough.

I refer to this mode of health as "ancient health." This is a mode of health where all needs of the spirit, mind and body—activity, food, sleep, are considered as one with the earth, in alignment with nature. All ramifications of an action are considered in virtually every aspect of life. I have truly learned to appreciate these people of old ways, and have developed an enormous amount of respect for ancient civilizations all over the world.

I became more aware of primitive ways after SynDee's car was totaled, and I sold my vehicle. An entirely new world opened up to me, one in which I had no idea how much I had been missing. It was the outside world.

I began to walk most places I needed to be. I quickly learned that energy really is precious. The food I was to eat was special in that it was literally "fuel for my vehicle." I found that I more fully grasped energy—all energy—as originating from the Earth, as sacred, precious, and as something not to be squandered.

Eventually, I began to ride my bike nearly everywhere I went. This did not feel as primitive to me as my feet, but I liked the feeling that I was consciously doing all that I could to respectfully conserve energy in riding my bike or walking. I lived each moment more completely; I was more present and aware of the constant exchange of energy. Individually to globally, from carbohydrates to electricity to gasoline, it *all* comes from the home that all people share. This realization was very enlightening. Each breath inhaled was in appreciation of life, creation.

Occasionally, I would stop at the local fruit stand on my way home from work to buy some fruits, veggies, and maybe some brown rice for dinner. I felt as if the gratitude that I felt was more profound than if I had stopped in my truck after work. The level of gratitude I felt approached the depth of gratitude our ancestors must have felt, in returning to their shelter with something to eat.

Yes, it sounds primitive. That's because it was, but I liked it. It is one more thing that felt so right. It was one of my ways of going back to basics, and try though I might, I could explain it to few people in a way that they appreciated it as I did. This was okay with me. It was clearly my own thing, seen as another quirk, but to me, something meaningful and significant, which I am grateful to have experienced.

BASICS

Humans have four basic needs. These are food, (including clean, fresh water,) shelter, (protection from extremes of temperatures and elements), clothing and love. When these basic needs are met, one can then consider their needs for creativity, self-expression, and amusement, recognizing that an individual's needs are unique; sometimes even moment-to-moment. My journey has taught me that an individual's health has largely to do with the proper balance (per individual) of two main things: food and sleep, not only the quantity of each, but the *quality* of the calories, and that *quality* of sleep. The two are equally important, and are completely interconnected. In my experience, less has to do with *quantity* of activity. I believe it has more to do with the *quality* of activity. I explain below.

FOOD

It's a no brainer: a person's health varies greatly merely by one's food choices. I find myself engaged in conversations regularly with different people about this. One man I often hear bragging, "I can eat anything I want. I eat about 3,000 calories a day, but then I go to the gym and pump iron for four hours, so I work it all off." I chuckle to myself because he says this as he is downing his second cheeseburger, with his fries and energy drink.

He has it backwards. The truth is, this man better hope that his tendons, ligaments, and muscles can withstand the four hours at the gym after work *over a prolonged time*, so that he doesn't become 500 pounds and truly obese. Is he truly doing his body a favor? I think not. He has big muscles, yes, but this Red Bull mentality is in no way promoting endurance, health, vitality. Furthermore, what is happening on the inside of his body? I would be nervous to sit with him at the doctor's office in waiting for his cholesterol results. His arteries, blood, cells, and heart, are working together very hard to deliver oxygen-rich blood to his exercising muscles. These organs are at the very core of life. They are essential to everything we do. Without these, there would be no bench presses or heavy squats.

I realized that society's general view of health is one of big muscles and impressive numbers on the outside. We pay little attention, and virtually pay little heed to our health on the inside. If our insides are full of junk, increasing our risk of heart disease, Diabetes, high cholesterol, there are no pushups, squats, and heavy bench press. There is not even time to reach into one's pocket to dial 9-1-1 when he/she is in cardiac arrest. At this point it is too late. This is really sad and yet, this is what is becoming more typical in today's western world.

I learned how important it was to truly nourish my body with plenty of nutrient- rich vegetables, fruits, whole grains, legumes and a few nuts and seeds. This provides more than enough calories and a sustaining balance of nutrients. This also eliminates the need to go to the gym for so long, spending an enormous chunk of already vanishing time, in unnatural conditions (fluorescent lighting, toxic indoor air, and overusing certain muscles.) This allows us the time and freedom to engage in activity we were designed for, not unnaturally intense, repetitive, and rigid "simulated" activity.

Chapter 13

I "Vegan"

My beginning point to wellness was when I became vegan. That is where I "vegan." It is an applicable and modern first step. I say this because as I speak of ancient people, no societies were vegan. Humans have a long history of eating meat. However, history is not without the "individual veg," who was healthy and happy for it. Naturally, the lifestyle of ancient people was more active, and they were able to use these calories.

This is why I came to the conclusion that eating a vegan diet, (reasons why I prefer the term "plant-based" are explained,) is a strong, balanced alternative in our modern world. People are very busy; we are always on the go. Let's face it: a sedentary lifestyle, combined with a diet of high fat, salty, food containing excess protein is disastrous to our health. Knowing this, I believe that a plant-based diet acts as a mitigating factor in today's modern world.

It is interesting that when I first began my plant-based diet, the pounds shed very quickly. I had not yet discovered the importance of activity. The pounds seemed to melt away, just by my being nourished with high quality calories. At this time, I was virtually still a "computer potato," always investigating a reptile, or a new plant online. I had also not yet discovered the value of my "unplugged" time, nor had I yet resumed my exercises, which I had enjoyed in 2001. By December 2009, after four months of eating exclusively plant-based, I was back to my weight in 2001, and this happened with not one single drop of sweat done in exercise.

My activity had not yet increased, and when I did begin to exercise again, it had little effect on my weight. In fact, I gained about five pounds, (probably of muscle mass) as muscle weighs more than fat. It was encouraging when this observation was later confirmed by one of my personal heroes, Dr. McDougall, in a lecture. The body, when nourished, regains balance and sheds the excess as it eliminates the junk, and finds its ideal weight. This is why I view a plant-based diet as a strong stance in today's modern world of increasing environmental destruction and declining health. Contrary to popular belief, a balanced, plant-based diet is good for humans. If high quality calories are consumed, it is what every cell in our bodies craves. In short, for me, my new path was a fine "beginning.

It was barely an entire week after beginning my new lifestyle that I noticed significant change. It was like stepping into a new realm or dimension. The door of fulfillment was then wide open. The difference in the way I felt for the better was more than the difference between night and day. It felt like stepping from the 114-degree Las Vegas heat in mid-July into an air-conditioned building of 70 degrees! It was that noticeable. The impact was that profound.

What's in a Word? Everything

Rip Esselstyn, author of The Engine 2 Diet and a triathlete, uses the term "plant-strong." In his book and presentations, this term replaces the word vegan. The change in perspective merely in a word is worth noting. In the strictest sense of the word, "vegan" refers to someone who avoids animal products in any form, while also refusing to contribute to the suffering of living beings as much as possible. In short, "vegan" seems to have automatic ethical implications, whereas the term "plant-strong" is fitting for a triathlete, one who understands health both from the inside and the outside. (See Engine2diet.com)

People come to their own truth, as they learn their own needs, at their own pace, and in their own way. I believe the word vegan automatically puts people on the defensive, both those who aren't, and perhaps even some who are. People may see it as something nice, but "untouchable", something that "I could never do." I believe revision is needed in how it is viewed both by vegans and those who are not. (This view may not apply as much in other regions, but this seems most fitting where I live.)

The general implication of Rip Esselstyn's term "plant-strong" is that it implies a choice of individual health, a diet "strong in plant foods." I choose to use the term "plant-based" as a substitute for the word vegan. I also consider the terms "plant-based" and "plant-strong" to be interchangeable. I believe this is a matter of preference, and one can expand into other terms, if and when asked.

I choose my terms carefully out of respect for each individual's journey. For instance, "plant-based diet" instantly implies that health is the primary reason for this diet, which is instantly less threatening to others. The concept of a plant-based diet for health is a lot less threatening to other people than is the concept of ethics, as implied with the word vegan.

Health does not put people on the defensive, as does the ethical argument, which is normally associated with the word vegan. Either of these terms, plant-strong, or plant-based, gently suggests one's awareness of conscious, individual responsibility and acknowledgement that *any* change, be it for health, the environment, or otherwise, must begin on an individual level. The term "plant-based" (or plant-strong",) to me says, "I love and respect myself enough as a person to take care of myself. Therefore, I choose to begin with this first, strong step of eating well." As mentioned by Esselstyn, a person can be vegan as it is traditionally defined, and avoid all animal products, but if they are eating nothing but white rice and tofu, then yes, their health will suffer dramatically, and in eating for health, they would be missing the basic fundamental of plant-based nutrition. Furthermore, in doing this, one is also missing a major fundamental of health: *caring for oneself.*

Personally, I choose my diet for health, lifestyle, and ethics. I love being healthy, but I also choose not to contribute to or support the suffering of animals and the destructive effects the meat industry has both on people's health and the planet, and the awful realities of meat production.

I began in 1994 as a vegetarian, but have since realized other benefits of a plant-based diet in preventing animal suffering. But it is important for all people to respect other individuals' lifestyle and food choices. We are all journeying. It is important to respect the individual pace and mode of growth and learning. Education regarding health and nutrition is far more powerful than arguing about small differences. People choose health and progress in their views, in their own way and their own time. Individual mode and pace must be respected.

Considering one's audience can serve well. People should be mindful how the word vegan sounds to others—impossible and untouchable, and for the average person, "it sounds good, but it's something I could never do," and to many others, it just sounds too extreme. As mentioned by Rip Esselstyn, the term "plant-strong" has no club to join, with shiny badges or membership cards. All are invited. No person will be kicked out of the club who chooses to wear leather, or for including honey in their food choices. Health, wellness, nutrition, and especially ethics are individual things. What may be right for one, at one time, may not be right for another. The terms plant-strong and plant-based accommodate this reality.

Health to Ethics, an Individual Thing

With all that said, I "vegan" the "cold tofu" method. (See the book <u>Vegan Freak</u>) For anyone considering it, my advice is to do what speaks to you. Do what calls you. Do it in your own way and at your own pace. I happen to be a very all or nothing kind of person. How could I do anything other than the cold tofu method? While you consider it, I suggest doing some research. (See my suggested reading and websites of interest section in the back of this book.) There is an ample supply of information available for those who wish to pursue this healthy path. There is much resistance, myths, and misinformation too. Do your research.

A plant-based diet should be chosen for the right reasons. There are many health benefits of a plant-based diet. Do what you can as you can, in a healthy way, and of respect for yourself. Do nothing out of fear, anxiety or worry. Fear is of low energy; it leads to more fear.

There may be a period of transition, where determination to live this way will be required. Never give up. As you will discover, this lifestyle should make people healthy and happy, not provide another reason to fight with one another. If one were to eliminate animal products from the diet, and replace it with soymilk, white rice and an occasional leaf of iceberg lettuce, this only invites malnourishment. Variety is always important with any choice of food, and is every bit as essential here.

A well-planned, nutritious diet of plant foods consists of many green, living vegetables. This includes many different colors, whole grains, (including quinoa, brown rice, legumes, fresh fruits, plenty of fresh water, some nuts, seeds and avocadoes. Food of this sort can and does taste great. The endless variety of produce, colors, textures, flavors, herbs and spices in different combinations are… well… endless. This lifestyle does not need to be, (and should not be,) one of deprivation or scarcity. As Dr. Joel Fuhrman says, "Eat to live!"

When I first became vegetarian in 1994, I did so strictly for my own health. I had made a bet with my older sister Lora, that I could "hack" the vegetarian diet after I had discovered her rice and soy milk one evening in the fridge. I wanted some, she didn't want to give me any; so she said, "that's special food for vegetarians, and you would never be able to handle it."

Of course, then I had to prove her wrong. I said, "Wanna bet?"

The bet was for two weeks. I tried it. I never went back. That was how much better I felt, eliminating only meat from my diet, as a junior in high school! Now, as I eat more and more plant strong, I feel a hundred fold better than I did as a vegetarian! I have lost my excess weight. My total cholesterol dramatically decreased. [See chapter 1.] There was another unexpected benefit: within days, my arthritis, and my "burning" in my shoulders and elbows faded away. My joints cooled down. The body begins to heal itself when we nourish it with the *right* things: healing, living nourishment.

ETHICS

I prefer to dwell on peace, happiness, and joy; however, it is difficult to discuss the eating of plant foods, versus animal foods without the topic of ethics entering the discussion as a factor at some point. There are several other books and websites that paint the awful reality of animals exactly how it is. I deliberately omit great detail here. However, it is worth noting not only how an animal dies, but how it lives prior to its death. Both of these factors influence the food, whether in the form of eggs, dairy, or meat.

Suffice it to say, that when the animals that we consume for food die, it is as if it were straight out of a horror movie. There is little to no consideration for their levels of pain, discomfort, or fear during death, or when alive, for that matter. All processes are designed to increase maximum profits, with virtually no regard for their life, or in taking it.

People who ask me about this often say, "It's going to die anyway." I feel that it is more awful the way the animal lived than the way the animal died… this says a lot, because their deaths are anything but pretty.

Again, guilt, fear, worry, regret are not good reasons to begin something new. This is why I choose not to dwell on the pain and suffering of animals. Does it affect me? Absolutely, I see the suffering of *any* being as awful, sickening, despicable, and incomprehensible. However, I believe that for *all* involved, love for the self, in desiring health, is a much kinder, far more effective approach toward a peaceful world where all coexist.

Neither blame, nor judgments have a place. We are all in and through our world together. A vegan would not be justified in blaming those who work in the front line at a meat packing plant, and vice versa. It is easy and tempting to place judgments on one another.

I have compiled a complete set of instructions for you when that becomes tempting: Don't.

We are all in this together. Let the change begin with you, and avoid the temptation on how much or how little everyone around you is doing. You start the change. One of my favorite quotes is from someone for whom I have developed the utmost respect, Mahatma Gandhi. "*Be* the change in the world you wish to see. "Again, do not dwell on the pain and suffering. It is self-defeating, and is guilt and fear-based…and it is just plain depressing. I believe it is important to not focus on pain, misery and suffering. When I first became vegan, just after reading <u>Diet for a New America</u>, both my health, and the awful reality of animals were reasons for me to change. Today, both reasons confirm my choice.

Early in my research on this diet, I was overwhelmed by the sensitivity I felt and the amount of focus I placed on the suffering of animals, and it was beginning to really dampen my mood and my spirits. As a wellness activist, in gently encouraging people toward health, hope and compassion helps me to cope with the pain I often feel for suffering animals. Personally, I prefer to believe that I am doing more for animals, as I keep happy, healthy, enjoy life, than if I were to become embittered.

I am grateful at my new found joy, health and happiness in eating a plant-based diet. I hope I'm doing some good in the world as I have chosen to cease the use of animals for food. I was glad to know that it is not necessary!

NUTRITION

In speaking of health and nutrition, I was relieved to hear that we do not need to eat animals or animal products to live. With only one exception, our bodies do not require any nutrient that cannot be found in plants. All essential nutrients are present in plants.

Arguably, the one vitamin we may need from an animal source is Vitamin B-12. Author, Rex Bowlby clarifies any potential confusion very informatively in his plant based diet guide, "Plant Roots: 101 Reasons the Human Diet is Rooted Exclusively in Plants. On the discussion of vitamin B12, Bowlby writes:

"Although it is the only vitamin not made by plants, it is not made by animals either. It is made by bacteria. The bacteria are found in the soil and stream water. It is also found in animals presumably by way of the soil and stream water. And it grows in the colons and mouths of humans."[1]

Bowlby calls this a test of faith by Mother Nature for vegans; Bowlby continues, "Much of the mystery of B12 has yet to be unraveled." Bowlby states in Plant Roots 101 that 95 percent of cases of B12 deficiency have occurred in non-vegetarians.

Our individual biochemistries and make-ups vary. This is one nutrient that advocates of the vegan diet often recommend supplementing. This includes Dr. McDougall. (See DrMcDougall.com)

Health Benefits of Nutrition

There exists a rather new term in the medical and insurance fields, one whose usage has become an accepted norm: "medical debt." It is a real term used to explain the hundreds of thousands of dollars, individuals or families rack up in an attempt to "get better" from all forms of ailments, from heart disease, to cancer, to many other terminal illnesses.

As mentioned earlier, the combinations of potential benefits of living "plant-strong," are too numerous to list here. The possibilities are endless. Here are some of the most outstanding.

---

1   Plant Roots, 101 reasons why the human diet is rooted exclusively in plants. By Rex Bowlby. P.84

Weight Loss:

A well-planned plant-based diet is a whole, healing, sustainable way to live. This diet should include both raw and cooked veggies, whole grains, legumes, wide variety of vegetables of all colors, both cooked and raw, brown rice, potatoes, sweet potatoes, and a few nuts and seeds. This is a whole and sustainable way to live.

Lowered Bad Cholesterol:

The plant-based diet also ensures that LDL or "bad cholesterol" will decrease and HDL or "good cholesterol" will increase. The avoidance of animal meat, eggs, and milk, is to avoid cholesterol. Cholesterol is not being consumed, as it would be in the typical western diet. Cholesterol is only found in animal products, meat, poultry, fish, cheese, eggs, and dairy products. It is not found in plants.

The human body also produces cholesterol in small quantities. Our bodies, being the amazing, healthy machines that they are, make HDL, or the healthy cholesterol with exercise. Knowing that our bodies make cholesterol in small amounts, we know that we have no external, nutritional requirement for it. We do not have to obtain it from our diets.

A well-planned plant-strong diet is also low in saturated fat. Early on, I was puzzled to learn of the difference between cholesterol and saturated fat. Cholesterol is not found in plants, whereas saturated fats are found in plants, although in much lower quantities than that found in animal foods, with the exception of palm oils, including coconuts. These are high in saturated fat. Saturated fat is solid at room temperature and is one of the major factors in heart disease and obesity, two of the major health epidemics in the world today.

Lower Toxicity:

Today, at the height of the digital age, and with the height of technological advances in every field toxins are part of virtually everything we do. They are impossible to avoid entirely, but minimizing them and their detrimental effects on our well-being *is* possible, as our bodies become healthier, and as we give them more of what they need, they are more able to assimilate these toxins. Higher dosages of toxins are found in the milk, eggs, fish and flesh of animals we consume. Toxins accumulate at higher doses in animals than in plants.

Animals that are going to be used as food are given heavy doses of antibiotics to kill the bacteria and contamination that are present under such filthy conditions. Antibiotics are not destroyed by cooking meat, as with bacteria. They find their way to our bodies. Residues of antibiotics are not good for us. Antibiotics are still toxins, even if we are sick and the doctor prescribes them to us, this does not make them non-toxic just because we are sick, or because they are prescribed by a doctor. Dr. Joel Fuhrman talks of this in his lectures.

There are also growth hormones given to the animals whose milk, eggs and flesh we consume. A larger animal means greater profits for agribusiness. In such industries, weight equates to profit. The faster and larger they can cause an animal to grow, the better it is for their profit margin. Growth hormones are added to increase weight. Science has only begun to discover all the ways that hormones are damaging to our health. They don't exactly help keep us trim. Think about it: a baby cow, at about two-hundred pounds, becomes a 1600-2000 pound animal, in approximately ten months; this is due largely to its mother's milk, which is designed to do just that—cause a large animal to grow even larger, as in ten short months! Neither substance is good for humans. Cow's milk is designed to make a calf huge very quickly. It is very capable of doing the same thing to us. Growth hormones are designed to.... well, you get the point.

I am only touching on the basics here; many books have been written on this very thing. I recommend Diet for A New America here by John Robbins. Robbins has done the research, talked the talk and walked the walk. An entire section of his book discusses this very topic of chemicals found in the animals we consume. I also recommend Plant Roots by Rex Bowlby, an informative book on this topic and others as well.

Hormones and antibiotics are not the only toxins affecting our bodies when eating meat, dairy and eggs of animals. There are many other harmful toxins, which accumulate at higher concentrations in the flesh, eggs and milk of animals. This process is called biomagnification or bioaccumulation, and it makes perfect sense when you trace toxins through the food chain. For example: a specific toxin is purchased to eradicate the grasshoppers in the garden. The garden pesticide is applied, and the grasshoppers are poisoned. Before the grasshopper actually dies of poisoning, it is caught and eaten by a mouse. The dosage permeating the grasshopper is not enough to kill the mouse, which may eat more toxic bugs. Therefore, the toxin accumulates in the cells of the mouse, and at a higher concentration than where it originated—the grasshopper. This mouse is later captured and eaten by an owl, or hawk, which now has ingested an even higher amount of the toxin than the mouse did. When it is considered that many harsh chemicals do not break down or absorb, many simply remain just as toxic with the passage of time, it is evident how this could affect our entire planet. The species at the top of the food chain are essentially the "catch all" for accumulating toxins. This occurs in all living things.

The bottom line is this: Toxins accumulate more rapidly and at a higher concentration in animal cells than in the cells of plants. Recently, I have wondered how many of my symptoms during mental illness were worsened by the toxins I was ingesting through my diet, which still depended highly on dairy and eggs.

Mental Clarity:

One of the greatest benefits for me was the clarity of thought which was completely new to me. It was as though the 'mental fog" of the past ten years, suddenly lifted, and the sun shone through again.

It is known that fewer cholesterol blockages in the blood vessels, equate to a more nutrient rich blood supply to the brain, helping one to think more clearly. (Dr. Dean Ornish mentions this in his lectures.)When the body is nourished and treated well, it is much better able to heal and repair itself.

There are theories as to the cause of mental illness, but the cause is unknown. For me, it was obvious that something was causing my brain to not work optimally. I believe my recovery was due to the positive changes in diet, acting as a "double punch." One, I was finally nourishing myself, by choosing to eat living plant foods loaded with vitamins, minerals, phytochemicals, all the things my body was in need of. I was eating nutrients that are far more concentrated in plants, which had a powerful cleansing and detoxifying effect. Second, I was replacing the "bad stuff, with the "good stuff," eliminating the highly concentrated toxins present in animal products. This was the "one two punch," which I believe proved so effective. In short, I eliminated the junk food, and replaced it with healing, nutrient rich, plant-based foods.

Nutrient Vitality:

Eating a vegan, plant-based, or as Rip Esselstyn says, "plant-strong" diet is more complete in all the essential nutrients our bodies need than is the standard western diet. Eating a variety of plant-based foods ensures more adequate vitamin and mineral absorption by the body. In this way, it is a more complete and more efficient way to eat. Plants contain abundant combinations of fiber, phytochemicals, antioxidants, vitamins, essential fatty acids, and minerals, all of the very things the human body so desperately needs. There are so many benefits to achieving a balance of all these compounds. They help to boost the immune system, allowing the body to better fight off infections and diseases. They help regulate hormonal balance, promoting weight loss when needed, they assist the body in restoring and repairing itself during deep sleep, they regulate brain chemistry, and they ensure lower levels of LDL cholesterol and blood pressure.

The current western diet, laden with animal products, meat, sugars, oils, fatty foods and highly processed food, is severely lacking in strong, healing nutrients. These foods, being high in animal products, also mean added fat and cholesterol. As mentioned earlier, it is also high in saturated fat, which is one of the major known culprits in people with high cholesterol and heart disease.

The typical western diet is also high in protein, in fact, too high. The amount of protein we require for wellness is far less than the typical western meal offers. Too much protein is a major factor in contributing to weight gain, osteoporosis, arthritis, diabetes, heart disease, kidney stones, and several cancers. Dr. Fuhrman spoke of this rather humorously in one of his lectures. After explaining the various complications, one can experience from these and other ills of the standard western diet, including heart surgeries, rectal probes, etcetera, with much laughter from the audience, he said, "I would rather …eat vegetables."[2] He said so much, in so few words, and yet, so simply.

---

2   Get Healthy Now! DVD Available at Vegsource.com

Eating a balanced, plant-strong diet ensures adequate vitamin, mineral, protein and fat intake as long as adequate amounts of calories are consumed.

Spirituality:

Of all the things I both researched and noticed about myself in my plant-based diet, spirituality is the most abstract and difficult to explain. This is a part of the path to self-discovery that is completely an individual's choice, naturally depending on how the individual perceives his or her experience. Anyone must choose their own path and discover all of the wonders that are part of health. It is something you must try for yourself and see what you discover. I submit that it will change your life.

Mahatma Gandhi said, "I do feel that spiritual progression demands at some stage, that we should cease to kill our fellow creatures for the satisfaction of our bodily wants." When I first read this statement, it shed light on some doubts. How can kindness, compassion, love, gentleness, harmony, and spirituality progress when I take the life of another being to satisfy my taste buds?

Judy Carman clarifies any confusion in her statement in her book Veggie Soup for the Chicken's Soul. She writes, "... It weakens the soul to participate in another's suffering." She goes on to say, "So veganism is a sacrament, a gift to the animals and to the environment, a protest, a daily prayer, and it is also the bedrock of spiritual bliss."

I noticed that I was more in tune with my own needs, nature, other beings, and my own spirituality. For me, it simply felt "right". This is not something I could explain, reason, or prove.

The Environment:

I do notice much talk these days about the environment, going green and nurturing the earth. I learned that one of the single-most effective things I can do to be more "eco-friendly" is to eat less meat and dairy. The production of meat is destructive for the environment. There is a humorous adage, which implies that a vegan Hummer driver is more beneficial to the environment than a Prius driver who eats meat.

I learned in my research that millions of gallons of water are used to raise the animals we consume. It is a highly inefficient way to attempt to sustain ourselves; twenty-five hundred gallons of water can raise one-pound of beef, or it can raise 40,000 potatoes. I am one who loves the Earth, and all of life. I am fascinated by life throughout the globe. The animals, plants, birds, trees, reptiles and insects of the earth have always intrigued me. I feel as though I am giving myself a gift in doing all that I can to help take care of the many species of birds, trees, mammals, reptiles, and fish that are within the scope of my influence.

The Entire Picture

For the first few months after my new change, I saw the veg diet as the only thing there was. It was sort of like looking beneath my magnifier loupe at the stamens of a flower; plant-based was all that I could see of what had helped me. This was where I put my focus. Now, as I take a few steps back, I can see the entire flower, each petal, its leaves, its stem, and the way in interacts with the natural world around it. This is the view I now prefer.

The adoption of a vegan diet was indeed a fine beginning for me, but I understand now that it was a stamen of the flower, although an essential phase and a fine beginning for my new path and new life, I now choose to see the entire picture, and how all aspects interact with it. It was one vital step, an essential part of the whole.

I have discovered several other aspects of wellness since that wonderful first step. I write about two of these below. They are sleep and activity.

Chapter 14

Sleep

I often use triangles as symbols. One of them that I use often as an object lesson is what I call "the wellness triangle." This is the balance theory of sleep, activity and high quality calories, which proved to be such a vital discovery during my journey to wellness. The foundation of an equilateral triangle is formed by the base at two points. These act as two points of wellness. They are high quality calories, and adequate sleep, both deep, and sufficient in length. The third point of the triangle represents activity. While exercise and activity is important, there is no need to exercise to exhaustion, (as once thought,) while eating high quality calories from plants and receiving adequate, regular sleep.

My newfound state of health is of the utmost importance to me; it is very important that I eat and sleep well to ensure well-being. I work hard to apply all the aspects of what I call the wellness triangle into my life. Of the three sides of this wellness triangle, (diet, sleep, and exercise), sleep has been the most difficult to find my point of balance and maintain consistently. I have closely observed myself throughout my sleeping patterns and have developed a theory about the regimen that works for me.

In my wellness triangle, the second and equally important aspect of health is deep, rejuvenating sleep. Most experts agree that good quality, deep, R.E.M. sleep is essential to good health.

I prefer to think of sleep as a uniquely individual time for important repair and rejuvenation. Why should we allow anything, or *anyone,* to interrupt this valuable time in any way? I believe that we should not; sleep should be a top priority in taking care of ourselves. Sleep is vital. Over time, I have kept close record of my own various sleeping patterns. I have tracked different patterns at different times, and how these all relate to the activities of the day. I have come up with this simplified formula: I wake up naturally without an alarm, and then I nourish myself with nutrient dense, healing foods throughout the day. I receive adequate amounts of activity throughout the day, and a lot of outside time, regardless of the season. When I adhere to this formula, I am rewarded with deep, rejuvenating sleep. I am still figuring things out. I am not yet where I would like to be regarding sleep. As mentioned earlier, it is the most challenging. However, I am taking great steps forward. I am aware of my needs, and as I need to, I make adaptations to my sleep environment, making it more conducive to sound sleep.

Often, I awake refreshed, invigorated and more prepared for the activities of the day. It is easy to see how activity, sleep, and quality of calories is very much a cycle; begin anywhere. How about when we first wake up: If one wakes up from a deep sleep gradually, with the natural increase of light, we are more prepared for the next part of our day, whether it is a bit of food, or a step outside to smell the morning air, or soaking in a few rays of the rising sun, or perhaps the cool rain on our face, or an early morning shower.

Our activities throughout the day greatly affect the quality of our sleep. Think about it, which would more likely contribute to sound sleep—a one-hour walk through a nature park, or a one-hour session on the computer? I found that outside time worked wonders for my sleep and my overall health too. I was grateful to discover my point of balance in this area. I learned through my own experience and careful tracking through my sleep diary that activity, particularly outside activity, was important for my quality of sleep. I originally had thought that I had to wear myself out in exercise to sleep well, but I have since learned that this is not true.

Activity and sleep are so paralleled in how one affects the other, that one cannot really be discussed without the other. One cannot really define where one begins, and one ends. This is because one so directly influences the other.

I observe that generally, people are too busy for exercise. This makes us sick of hearing of the importance of it. It is seen as a separate, (although necessary) extension of life. When I first realized this, I was very annoyed by it. I was very busy with work, and trying to cram in extra things such as exercise was just too much, and was frankly stressful.

Time outside is vital to our make-up as humans. Receiving natural light affects our cycles, our rhythms, which are deeply rooted within our genetic memory, recorded since our beginnings. These cycles are as old as the earth itself. They affect us more than we may realize. Surviving today's hustle and bustle has taught us to ignore these cycles, deny our instincts, and numb the symptoms of our disturbed existence.

I often reflect on one summer morning in September 2009, I took a bike ride. It was the last time I rode my bike until I got it out as my primary mode of transportation in the spring of 2011. This bike ride was something I was trying to cram in before I had to leave for work. I was riding my bike among beautiful surroundings, trees, birds, the river view, not realizing how much I needed these things and how much I loved being among them. The thought occurred to me with great irritability as I rode: "We are the only century throughout the entire human history that needs to exercise as a separate and extra part of their lifestyle!" I was quite irritated. Needless to say, this particular bike ride didn't help me to wind down, and I felt more stressed going to work that day than if I had stayed at home and skipped the exercise.

That bike ride proved to be an epiphany however. Throughout human history, whether hunting, gathering, or fetching water for survival, our ancestors' exercise needs were met naturally, as was their need for sunshine and time outside. It was all part of their lifestyle!

In our modern world, we go to work for nine or more hours a day. We have the same needs as our ancient predecessors. However, we now replace and supplement those needs with modern forms of activity—perhaps working at a desk, or in a warehouse, factory, or kitchen. When we finally get home, often there is little daylight left, but we are still trying to find time to exercise, which is crucial for health. This is what both baffled and irritated me. I began to think of ways that I could implement activity into my lifestyle—naturally. Again, our sleep and activity, act for us on an influential relationship. One always influences the other.

Just as activity affects the quality of sleep, sunshine, natural light also improves the quality of sleep. One reason outside time is so important for health is the benefit of sunshine. It is essential to our well-being. Sunlight

OWEN STAPLES

helps our bodies produce vitamin D. Experts understand more all the time the important role this substance has on our body.

My thought was one of irritation, but also realism. It went something like, "It's 2011, and *who* has time to exercise, after nine or more hours in the office, factory, classroom, or kitchen? No one! If they had some extra time, that person would have to consume four energy drinks just to *want* to pull themselves off of the couch, myself included."

In this age, we are very busy. It is a fast paced world; it almost seems as if we must choose one or the other, activity and exercise, (both terms used here interchangeably,) or a busy lifestyle. More often it seems the case that it is too much to do both. It is increasingly difficult to find time to exercise and this is a major problem because exercise is so essential to our well-being! We must find time for some activity. Activity does not have to be intense or especially long, as is commonly assumed. Remember the man who boasted of his three-thousand calories a day? Instead, moderate activity such as raking leaves, a walk with the dog, or a hike is essential. So generally speaking, we work in the office, warehouse, kitchen, or classroom all day. We receive very little natural light, and sunshine. We do not exercise either, and therefore our quality of sleep is reduced drastically. This is where the use of the triangular model for wellness illustrates the reciprocal relationship of sleep, food, and activity well.

After I sold my truck, I rode my bike to work out of necessity at first. But I quickly found that I really enjoyed riding my bike to work. Whether riding my bike or taking the bus, or sometimes a combination of both, I received some time outside, and some activity too. I came to value and enjoy the variety, stimulation, fresh air, and decompression time. This proved to me that there are modern ways of meeting our activity needs as a naturally blended part of life in a way that fits and balances effortlessly with all the many facets of life.

When I did this, I felt great in many ways. On an environmental level, I knew that I was helping to eliminate pollution, if only by not contributing to it, while on a physical level, I was meeting my need for exercise. Mentally, it gave me a small daily reprieve from the "rat race".

Whether I ride an hour here, or twenty minutes there, my needs for cardio workouts are met. Occasionally, I walk to a nearby nature trail. Between the walking and the biking, I enjoy a varied balance between moderate and intense cardio workouts. Naturally, some workouts are more intense than others. This would depend on my intensity I choose to exert and the incline of the hill I face. As with anything, variety is good. Balance is good. I acquire both… naturally.

I perform some calisthenics. I aim to do these twice weekly. If I miss a workout or two, I'm not overly concerned. I just pick up where I left off the next time I can. I try to work out every major muscle group in my body twice a week with strength training. I own very few weights by choice. To me, these would only equate to clutter in my space and in my life. This is how I prefer it. I am not interested in being large and bulky; therefore I don't need a gym membership.

I also perform stretching exercises as part of my nightly wind-down routine on weekdays. Not only is this recommended for anyone after a workout, it also happens to improve my sleep by helping my muscles to relax. What a coincidence!

This is how I prefer it. I eat well on living, plant-based, plant-strong foods, receiving not only a balanced supply of nutrients, but also adequate caloric intake for my activity level. The calories are high quality and nutrient-dense. There are no extra "filler" calories. There is no need to go to the gym after work and "pump some iron." My lifestyle has been my "gym" throughout the day. This is my concept of "ancient health" in action. It is slightly modified for our modern world, but the concept is intact.

Chapter 15

All Creatures

One less-expected factor which impacts our health is appreciating other creatures, whether in nature or some of the ones we call pets. This aspect of health affects every facet—the physical, mental, and spiritual, and yet we hear about it less frequently than factors such as sleep, exercise and diet.

Think of a childhood pet that you adored. If you didn't have a childhood pet, recall a time when a butterfly's freedom and colors spoke to you in a way that nothing else could, or maybe a time when the first sound you heard in the morning was the pleasant song of a bird? There is a special exchange that occurs when we stop to appreciate other living beings. This exchange can take place from a distance in nature, or from the loved ones who share our couch, our pets. I think we all have a living being somewhere in our life that we can appreciate and love on many levels.

Angela Hynes, in a March, 2005 issue of Natural Health, p.75, sums up my point beautifully. She writes, "Of course, anyone who shares a home with a pet—be it furred, feathered, finned, or scaled—knows that animal/human interaction fosters well-being. Evidence of this healthy connection fills books, cable TV shows, and now medical journals. Over the last few years, researchers have discovered that owning a pet can reduce blood pressure, heart rate, and cholesterol, lower triglyceride levels, lessen stress, result in fewer doctor visits, and alleviate depression."

Science is only scratching the surface of understanding the many benefits of having animal companions in our lives. This is apparent when petting or viewing a beloved companion animal. Many of our worries, fears, and stresses diminish.

PLANTS

"…and green plants, they've got mad life they're sentient.
They're as beautiful as you and they *like* to dance." -311

As with appreciating or sharing our homes with animals, there is something also therapeutic about plants. Whether in the garden, yard, or in a single room dwelling, plants offer a type of nourishment and fill a certain void. During my bout with mental illness, I can recall many times where simply gazing at one of the houseplants with which I felt a connection and which I did my best to care for, lifted my spirits, calmed my tension, and I experienced an overall ease of my senses. I was filled and nourished in those moments.

Appreciation of plants and animals implies our need for interaction with the natural world. I believe some of us need this more than others; but all of us can benefit from this type of nourishment, to one extent or another.

If I ride my bike or walk to work, I receive exercise, outside time, interacting with the birds, grass, trees, flowers, clouds, mountainous scenes, sky and sun. I arrive at work more prepared for what I may be doing with my mind free and clear. I arrive home after work more at ease and the major bonus: I had my exercise and health dosage for the day. I also saved money because I didn't use any gas for a vehicle, no wear and tear on that vehicle, and I don't have to buy a gym membership. When I arrive home, I feel free—free to give of my time and myself to my loved ones. I have given *to* myself; now in turn, I have *something* to give back.

There are times when extreme temperatures, or extremely poor air quality make exercising outside unsafe. During these times, I get my exercise indoors where I am surrounded by my houseplants and companion animals. This is contributing to other aspects of wellness.

The spirit-mind-body connection is inseparable and undeniable. The state of one always influences the other. The body needs food, the mind needs stimulation, but also rest, the spirit needs nourishment and nurturing care. The entire being thereby is nourished, aided, as its needs are considered. Attaining synchronicity here is desired.

Chapter 16

What is green?

"The beauty of Green is where light is now
broken by what it touches…" -311

There is a lot of talk about eco-friendly and going Green these days. It is common to see and hear of people saying, "Go Green." Taking the green movement into our homes seems to have become a fad.

It is obviously a good thing that there is an increasing interest in respecting the environment, but I suggest that this must be genuine, and not perpetuated as a marketing scheme. As a marketing scheme, I have two words which sum up the way I feel about this very nicely. They may surprise you. "Gag me." Yes, you read those words, (five letters) correctly. To me this says, "All you have to do to reverse any environmental destruction is screw in a compact fluorescent bulb, buy a bamboo floor, or buy a car which receives twenty mpg instead of ten, and all is A-OK."

I do believe that many people are genuinely concerned for the environment, for which I am most grateful. However, my gripe is with the way retail interests are exploiting this genuine concern all for a profit. The underlying message that costs millions of dollars to reach people is, "You have to spend a lot of money buying green products from us, and then you don't have to make any real changes that might be inconvenient. Just buy the light bulbs!"

I am a botanist and a naturalist, and I happen to love the diversity of flora, habitat and fauna of this beautiful planet. I am not alone. I am grateful to so many people who share this appreciation for the life and beauty of earth. Just as many people do, I happen to have a lot of energy personally invested in caring for our home. I love our planet Earth.

I think that any attempt to take care of our home, whether genuine or just "going through the motions", is a good thing. I have softened my stance on this considerably. However, I believe it is important for all people to learn about the adages and causes they support. It is vital for everyone to approach the green movement with their eyes wide open, armed with accurate information. "Going Green is no longer seen just for the "tree hugger types." It is no longer deniable that we all share the same planet, and everything we eat, drink, buy, drive, wear and build comes from it, in one form or another. If all are to have enough, it is time for us to all come together to ensure this.

Previously, I have noticed corporations jumping on the "green wagon" at every turn. In my opinion, this is a classic case of not accepting responsibility, these entities that publicly proclaim the green steps they are taking as they tell others to "go green", and then offset their own eco-friendly approach by their other non-green practices. In these instances, what I really I hear corporations saying is, "We are aware that the rope is burning at both ends, but we are not interested in extinguishing the flame, only in slowing it down. Extinguishing the flame entirely would cause us to lose too much money. The next generation can worry about that."

I say let's keep "green" "eco-friendly" pure, with a genuine interest in taking care of our home. Let us not allow these adages to become motivated by greed. "Green" should never become a trendy marketing scheme, another way to make lots of money; only further contributing to the rapid combustion of the burning rope. If we are going green, we must be interested in extinguishing the flame of the burning rope. I say let us first completely extinguish the flame, and *then* lay the foundation of pure green as the new standard, one that is rooted in being genuinely committed to our home. I am grateful to be able to say that in the past two years, I have seen positive change in this way. I believe there is much to be optimistic about. We must come together, and be smart in doing so. We can do this!

PURE GREEN

I quote from one of my favorite houseplant books <u>Indoor Plants</u>, by Halina Heitz, "Also not to be undervalued is the positive effect that green plants have on us. Green is the color human beings need most. Its nature is peaceful, it banishes depression, and it has a relaxing effect. This is not surprising when you know that the lenses of our eyes do not have to adjust for green as they do for other colors."

In my home state of Utah there lives a large grove of Aspen trees, botanical name *Populus tremuloides*, nicknamed "Pando." Pando is the largest living organism on the face of the earth. These trees are clearly able to withstand the test of time. This wonder of nature began with one tree! At 80,000 years old and 6 million kilograms, (6,613.9 tons) this is the heaviest, and oldest living organism on the face of the earth. It is a *survivor*. Its extensive, massive root systems, which extend safely and deeply into the earth, have allowed them to survive 80,000 years of drought, pestilence, and forest fires.

I believe we can learn metaphorically from Pando. With our own roots planted firmly and extending deeply into the earth, over time, our thirst for nourishment, living water, and knowledge can preserve us and help us to survive droughts, forest fires, floods and the like. When the soil nearer the surface at times becomes toxic or corrupt, we can, at this point remember our roots, which all connect so deeply in the earth, able to access true nourishment and life-giving water. So yes, go green; but go green like *Populus tremuloides,* and be not swayed by corruption, the surface toxicity. Let Green remain pure, genuine, effective, deliberate, and conscious.

Chapter 17

"...and a little child shall lead them."

"Your health account is your wealth account." -Jack Lelanne

As I explained earlier, choosing health and the environment proved to have positive benefits for my finances too. I later discovered that this phenomenon has a name. "The Green Triangle" as spoken of by Ernest Callenbach. In Callenbah's theory, if I changed one side of the triangle, the other two sides were always influenced. It didn't matter if I began from finances, environment, or my own health; the other two were always influenced. Callenbach's Green triangle model demonstrates that if one takes steps in truly improving their health, it also improves the environment and areas of one's finances also. Note: This is different than my own triangle, the Wellness Triangle, which reciprocally connects high quality calories, sleep, and activity.

I discovered that when I walked or rode my bike, I didn't use any gas, and therefore I didn't contribute to air pollution and did not lose money to the gas pump. I discovered how great I felt in every way by making these two things, my health and the environment, my priority. It was always amazing to me how paralleled these two things were—whenever I acted on one, it influenced the other.

I found that the Green Triangle worked for me throughout my life in regards to the triangle's three main aspects: my state of health, the environment, and my finances. Our choices regarding any one of these three things have a ripple effect and always influence the other two facets.

I have kept this in mind as I have seen money come and go into my own life and the lives of others. I have observed ways in which our habit of spending a lot of money influences other areas of life, in obvious and less expected ways, as explained in the following pages. During my time at the hardware store, I had seven years to observe while performing my work. Granted, my perspective and lens changed many times during that period, but all observations combine as part of the journey.

Some of my most recent observations have been children and their relationship to money, both directly and indirectly. Through those many years I spent in the garden department of the hardware store, I spent a great deal of time among flowers, plants, trees, garden supplies, with a whole lot of outside time. I have noticed how children seem so naturally attracted to the natural world. If given a choice, and more likely, even if not given the choice, they will choose the flowers, trees, flowing fountain water, insects, and pigeons playing in a puddle. Children love life and they are almost able to "smell" it and seek it out. Many times, I observed children trying to play with the pigeons or wanting to help water the flowers. They clearly preferred this to going with their parents to the patio furniture, appliances, or the power tools section of any store.

Children naturally adore the natural world. They sense its life force; of course they do. Children, from birth to roughly twelve or so years of age, are more in tune than most adults, and if we were to look back on this age of our own lives, we would discover the same thing—we were more in tune with nature during this time of our lives than any other time. Why is this? I'm sure there are many factors, but I personally believe that beyond these ages we become desensitized, and it becomes easy for our lives to be consumed by unnatural, materialistic things. We become more and more concerned about money, how to make it, how to spend it, and less concerned with the natural wonders of the world. I say this is backwards.

Is it possible to maintain this in-tune state all of our lives? Absolutely. It requires, well… becoming as a little child, just as is written throughout several religious and spiritual writings. Let's not confuse child-like with childish.

I believe the natural attraction kids have toward the natural world should be encouraged. After all, being in nature, or surrounded by representations of it is wonderfully healing; it is therapeutic.

At the hardware store, it seemed as if children who wanted love and life sought it first where they knew they could find it—in the natural world. As their parents browsed other areas of the store, their children would search out a small section of "naturalness" and life. When their parents scold them upon finding them, irritated for wandering off, the children become confused.

I observed that they are often faced with confusion in regard to money from the beginning. It seems almost as if children desire to grow up so that they can have some freedom and self-expression. On the other hand, parents long for their childhood days, where they didn't have so much stress, responsibility and worries about money. I witnessed an inevitable conflict of interest: family relationships conflicting with money relationships.

I have seen people wildly spend their money on non-necessities, in almost an attempt to be free, and once again find innocence, peace and happiness. Their children are sometimes brought along as an alternative to hiring a babysitter. They become bored, immediately associating money with places they would rather not be. In short, they're not "buying it." They seek out the pigeons drinking from the water puddles, the trees, water fountains and flowers.

When I observed this, it was easy to see why there are increasing problems in society, and how our relationship with money is closely connected to these issues. I have witnessed many things that seem to confirm this.

Both as a consumer and because much of my working life was spent in retail stores, I have had firsthand exposure to people's relationship with money. We are encouraged to buy, buy, buy, and spend all that we have and then even more. Our young children become bored with all the shopping and mania. They have not yet developed the insatiable appetite for materialistic things—a walk in the park or a game of catch with a parent would still be their number one choice for activity. Throughout my working years, I have seen some children become lost, wandering off, seeking their own entertainment. I have unfortunately witnessed situations of verbal abuse as their guardians became mean toward a child who felt displaced. I have also witnessed times when children were left unattended which sometimes led to dangerous situations.

It is true that it takes a certain level of money in this day and age to live comfortably. However, I do believe that our obsession with money affects other areas of our lives, which we may not have considered, including our relationships. I believe we must start to make a choice to re-set our priorities.

Despite the disturbing things I have witnessed, I have also had the pleasure of experiencing beautiful, nurturing experiences. One mother and her son in particular stands out as a bonding experience where they were truly "building something together." I was working in another department on the opposite end of the store from the garden center when I had the pleasure of speaking to a mother and her son, who looked to be age eleven or twelve. Upon approaching them, I could immediately tell that this wasn't the typical situation. The mother, in a rich, Argentine accent explained that she and her son were building a birdhouse together. I glanced down at the cute boy. I couldn't quite tell if it was what he wanted or he was "just along for the ride." The more I observed in that first five seconds, the more I believed that his theme was: "I don't understand what this is all about, but my mom is excited and she is spending time with me, so here I am." This intrigued me.

I asked him if he preferred the birdhouse or the bird feeder. He replied the birdhouse. I was in the process of showing them the various types of nuts and bolts available with variances on how their piece could be attached.

As I watched their interaction and their discussion, and the amount of involvement and energy that each was giving this project, my interest was piqued. I knew I was witnessing something unusual, but beautiful nonetheless. I felt honored to play a small role in this.

Early in the flowing conversation, I had become overwhelmed with emotion, so much so that I found myself pursing my lips in an attempt to hide the quiver building in them. She was explaining the project to me, and as she took a few moments to study the details of hardware, I also glanced down briefly, in an attempt to hide the tears, then filling my eyes, doing my best to fight them back. I was relieved at an opportunity to look away briefly to collect myself as we walked a few aisles back to show them some possible options for birdhouse kits and bird feeders. I walked a few feet in front of them, by this time fighting extra hard to hold back the tears. I turned around briefly, having my tears under control, and asked the boy as casually as I could, "What is your favorite kind of bird?"

Without hesitation, and with almost no thought, he replied, "A parrot." I laughed out loud at his innocence. "I wish we had parrots here too, but I'm afraid you'll have to settle for magpies and sparrows here."

He smiled shyly.

I showed them the variety of birdhouse kits available; they chose carefully, and chose together. She asked him which he preferred and he pointed. They both thanked me and went on their way. I watched them walk away; then with a few tears which had forced themselves to the surface running down my face, I smiled warmly as I watched them contentedly walking together with their birdhouse. The boy turned around, and in his own cute, chubby way, waved and smiled shyly as if with gratitude.

That was it for me. I walked briskly to the bathroom, locked myself in the nearest stall, and the tears that I had held back for so long were allowed to fall, and fall they did; for quite some time, I allowed myself to just sob. I was so deeply touched by this precious unfolding. I was touched and grateful to also be allowed a very small part in it. It gave me hope. Here was this middle aged mother who didn't have a lot of money, but who still was doing more for her son than many parents who were very wealthy, financially speaking.

Perhaps she knew of the profound effect she was having on her son's life, teaching him about some basics of life, and if so, bless her soul. If not, still, bless her soul. That boy will forever have that experience to reflect upon, that of building something with his mother. I believe that he will recall it when he really needs it.

Chapter 18

The Circle of Truth

A circle is a perfectly round, flat sphere, with neither beginning nor end. This circle can represent our progression through change. If you only begin, it matters not where you start. Just start. This is all you need. Enjoy the journey and allow the circular flow of progression to gently carry you. You will naturally progress to the next step when you are ready. Just like the consistent, gentle, yet constant, cyclic flow of a circle. Once you begin, you will continue to progress…. naturally.

Shapes among living things are gentle circles, ovals, whereas squares, rectangles, or shapes with harsh, hard, energy-halting angles rarely exist among living things. When they do, gentler angles, or sometimes hairs, as seen in certain plant families for example, soften them. The rectangle of truth sounds rather ridiculous does it not? Balance, flow, harmony, and consistent progression are the ways of the natural world. I believe there are far more clues to a better way for us to be found in nature than we may have previously considered.

Truth is simple, not complex. We are often the ones who try to twist and complicate the simple nature of truth. Like a globe, it has no beginning and no end. The circle continues on its eternal round and the truth in and of itself is a cycle. This is truth, having no beginning and no end.

May I suggest the existence of a creative force, or higher power? It is the same Higher Power that hears all of our positive wishes, prayers, and longings of the soul. Whichever the preferred title for these utterances, in the end, they are communication with a power, which we either perceive, or for which we hope. Regardless of the differences in our views of this creative force, this force speaks a universal language, and is likely far less concerned with the minute details than we are.

A good friend once told me that the universe loves gratitude. I don't know if that wording is her own or from another source, but it always struck me as profound in its simplicity.

During my journey, one of the most important realizations I gained from my own recovery was that it is okay to honor and revere a creative force, or higher power, in a way that was comfortable for me. I realized that I mattered here; and that I had an essential role to play, simply by my unique individuality and the power of my choices. This new perspective of a spiritual relationship seemed to channel my healing and bring all else into focus. It was a nice seal to my newfound happiness.

After I had experienced health and happiness, as with any new thing, I was eager to allow spillage of the excess to help others. I loved my new life, the way I looked and felt, and I was interested in allowing others a taste of this new, life-giving water.

Please consider here with me a different world; as you read, visualize, be willing to set aside our global and individual differences, and see ourselves for what we are—human beings. There is one word upon which I think we can all agree that spirituality and religion is based, at the core of their teachings. This word, love, settles any conflict more resoundingly than others.

As you read, journey with me now me into a realm of how things *could* be, into a place that *is* within our grasp.

I have joy, high hopes, and optimism for where I imagine humanity journeying into light, life, and abundance. I want it. I want it for me. I want it for you. I want this peacefulness for all.

Be willing to slow down as you visualize a world where all beings have food, love and life. All have enough. All are, in every way, nourished. Neighbors help each other prepare for the storms of life. Neither individuals nor nations are at war with others; instead all synchronize in cooperation and harmony, individually to collectively, locally to globally. Among our top priorities are our planet and our health. We realize that the health of the two blends very well, they are mutually supportive, reciprocal.

Children, healthy and vibrant, are laughing innocently in the sunshine at their make believe games, completely oblivious to time, as they coax their faithful animal companions to tag along behind them. You can inhale with full breaths the crisp, clean air; it fills your cells with nourishment.

It is quickly apparent that there is very little crime. Disease is also greatly reduced and is no longer inevitable. Greed, racism, hate, war, fear, negativity, pain and suffering are only a distant memory of our former life.

We only know cooperation, love, equality, compassion, optimism, and gratitude for the grand level of health and vitality that we feel. For we all now know that we are equal and together, living in cooperation, sharing our planet. The trees, green and vibrant, offer fruits of all kinds. We no longer race to or from. There is no need; for there is no distress over money or jobs. Since each now has enough, we know that there is no longer a need for our frantic pace. The Earth is returning to its full vigor, and it is able to sustain food, water, and air in abundance. There is enough for all, and we know there always will be. Abundance is now the essence most apparent. Doubt and fear, originating from lack and scarcity, no longer have a place. We have jobs, but they don't consume our lives. This is a life nicely balanced between leisure and duty, work and play, together time and alone time, and we are engaged with helping others where it is needed.

Maybe you find yourself in magical wonder, as you pause to absorb the gentle gaze of a robin, or a squirrel; this touches your soul in a deep way. There is no longer enmity between humans and the creatures that fly, swim, crawl, walk, hop, or slither. You may pause and allow the colorful array of a hummingbird or butterfly; its cheery colors seem to greet you warmly, filling you.

This world of which I speak offers a new standard. Cooperation is a global priority, ensuring all are fed, nourished, clothed and housed. This they are. We fully understand that all the life on, in, and through the planet is sacred, and is here for a purpose, to help maintain balance.

All have enough; our simple lives are our own version of enough, and this fills us beyond capacity. Others always benefit from the excess spillage as our "cups runneth o'er." Selfishness or hoarding does not exist because all have their "satisfied enough".

Kindness abounds. We are supportive of one another, not only serving where there is a need, but also preventing the need in the first place. There is no deprivation or want, because the basic needs are prepared for and met before the need is created. This state of existence is all-inclusive. There are no feelings of exclusion, or of being left out. There is abundance in every form, for every being.

A sense of community and interdependency fills our consciousness. People may gather in safety, health and happiness, or they may choose to enjoy the peace of being alone, enjoying the rain from their inside window's view, or among the vibrant trees, surrounded with peaceful sounds of crickets, tree frogs, and birds.

Our thoughts are full of gratitude to one another, our animal companions, the beauty of the earth and trees, our fields of bountiful harvest of grains, wholesome, organic vegetables, and fruits of all kinds.

Pure, flowing water is abundant for us to use freely. We use it often for many things; it is seen as a sacred element, which sustains life. We sense the purifying effect it has on our souls. We cherish our relationship with this life-giving, life-sustaining element.

Our new abode here, in such a state of tranquility and perfect balance of health enables us to think optimistically more often. We are not paralyzed by fear and stress. We are able to do what we *choose* to, and do what matters the most to us. There is time and means for this now. You have time to be with your children, or your companion animals, as the forgotten memories return to you of how revitalizing in its simplicity a game of soccer outside or a snowball romp can be. It is at this time, you wonder in amazement to yourself why it took you so long to arrive at this beautiful, tranquil state. Then slowly you remember that this is how it was designed to be all along. You are not surprised. It is completely familiar. The answers, the memories wash through you like a gentle wave.

Laughter, divine and joyful, is ready to burst forth in outward expression. We know it is okay to laugh, and to cry too, even if both at the same time.

Even as an adult, you find yourself in the snowball romp or soccer game, or kick the can with your beloved children and/or companion animals, expressing yourself in an innocent outburst of fun, joyful laughter that you cannot hold back any longer. The feeling of joy and peace is unmistakable. You laugh with your children, just as you have seen your children do in pure innocence. You remember watching them do so in the past, when you experienced a sort of longing for that innocence once again. Well, here it is. You have earned it, and you know that it is ok to laugh, and you do so as you never have before. You relish the moment as the special one that indeed it is.

Vanished is the role with script we played in our families and societies. For we have learned to express and create for ourselves, offering our own unique gifts. We are no longer boxed in by the expectations placed upon us by the other actors in the play—for they are all freed too. We have all abandoned the script, and we watch in wonder as the most amazing story unfolds. All are satisfied, content, peaceful and truly happy.

There you are with your children, companion animals, dearest loved ones, surrounded by green grass, blue sky, bright flowers, swaying trees, clean air, breath-taking scenery, and with everything you love and hold most dear. Right in this moment, in its perfect simplicity, not all things are present and yet, nothing is lacking. You feel nourished, satisfied, whole and complete.

With gratitude, you know that this *can* last, and will. This state of tranquility and peace, which, your soul has always longed for, is finally here. It is here to stay.... always.

It is the way it was meant to be all along.

And so it is.

CONCLUSION

There you have it: a recipe for a better world. I'm a regular man who was willing be my own test subject. Apparently, I passed the test, but most of all, the tests passed! I tried it, worked it, walked, talked, hiked, climbed, crashed, cried, laughed; and here I am with a formula—one that works!

I thank you for journeying with me. I do appreciate your time and energy. Perhaps the main question on your mind is whether these things should be taken more as metaphorical, or literally. Don't give this dilemma too much energy. If you are wondering this, again, I have a question for you: Consider all spiritual or religious writings. Were they metaphorical or literal? Don't be troubled here on which you believe. The bottom line: How about you *choose* a combination of *both* that works for you. After all, as we consider any religious or spiritual writings, modern or ancient, are there lessons to be learned from both metaphors and literal interpretations? Absolutely.

You may be wondering if I am serious. The short answer: Yes, I am. I'm still here after all was said and done, and I re-affirm everything that I have said in the previous pages. Health and Happiness are a choice.

If you think and re-think, and still it is a lot to swallow, I have a simple beginning question for you: How seriously do you take your health and happiness, your finances, and your home-the Earth? Go from there.

Thank you for reading.

-Owen, the Naturalist.

THE END

Appendix

This is a brief list; but the resources are nearly endless. These are my favorites. I am not the expert; the listed books and websites below represent those people who are.

Research, research, research. I cannot emphasize this enough. Learn for yourself. Strong education is key.

The list below includes experts who have written books, produced DVD's, and websites, or all of the above, ranging from architects, to doctors, to authors, to nutritionists, to firefighters. I hope you enjoy learning and researching as I did. I read thirty-four books in fourteen months. Below are the experts who have done the research, can talk it, because they walk it.

SUGGESTED READING ORGANIZED BY TOPIC:

SPIRITUALITY
There's A Spiritual Solution to Every Problem by Dr. Wayne W. Dyer
The Power of Intention by Dr. Wayne W. Dyer
Veggie Soup for the Chicken's Soul by Judy Carman
The Care and Feeding Of Indigo Children by Doreen Virtue Ph.D.

SIMPLICITY
Less Is More by Cecile Anderews and Wanda Urbanska
The Heart of Simple Living by Wanda Urbanska
Un-jobbing by Michael Fogler
Feng Shui in a Weekend by Simon Brown
The New Good Life by John Robbins

DO YOUR OWN THING
Career Renegade, how to make a great living doing what you love by
  Jonathan Fields

PLANT BASED NUTRITION AND HEALTH
Food Revolution by John Robbins
The Engine 2 Diet by Rip Esselstyn
A Diet for a New America by John Robbins
Skinny Bitch by Rory Freedman and Kim Barnouin
Skinny Bastard also by Rory Freedman and Kim Barnouin
Healing Environments by Carol Venolia
101 Reasons Why I'm A Vegetarian by Pamela Rice
Vegan Freak by Bob and Jenna Torres
Plant Roots: 101 Reasons Why the Human Diet Is Rooted Exclusively In
  Plants by Rex Bowlby
Eating In the Light by Doreen Virtue Ph. D and Becky Prelitz M.F.T. R.D.
Food for the Future by John Gribbin

ANIMALS
Animal Liberation by Peter Singer
Animals and the Afterlife by Kim Sheridan
Animal Theology by Andrew Linzey

ENVIRONMENT
If You Love This Planet by Helen Caldicott, M.D.
Go Green Live Rich: 50 Simple Ways to Save the Earth (and get rich
  trying) by David Bach

LAW OF ATTRACTION
Excuse Me Your Life Is Waiting by Lynn Grabhorn
Three Magic Words by U. S. Andersen

NOVELS WRITTEN IN PARABLE FORM
The Celestine Prophecy by James Redfield
The Celestine Prophecy an Experiential Guide by James Redfield
Ishmael by Daniel Quinn

FINANCES
Total Money Makeover by Dave Ramsey (The get out of debt specialist)
Daveramsey.com

WEBSITES OF INTEREST
Self-sufficiency, enjoying outside and primitive living skills:
Codylundin.com
Wildflowers-and-weeds.com
Discovertheforest.org

HEALTH AND NUTRITION WEBSITES
Vegparadise.com
Drfuhrman.com
Engine2diet.com
Drmcdougall.com
Earthsave.org
Vegsource.com
Vegparadise.com
Healthforcenutritionals.com

SELF HELP
Wellbaskets.com

ANIMALS
Farmsanctuary.org
Animalsandtheafterlife.com
Kimsheridan.com

MENTAL HEALTH EDUCATION AND SUPPORT
Nami.org

My projects
www.naturalreptiles.com
www.wellnessdiaries.com
Life Is Conscious